RELIGIOUS WOMEN AND THEIR HISTORY

In memory of Ann Taylor
(1956–2003)

RELIGIOUS WOMEN AND THEIR HISTORY

Breaking the Silence

Editor

ROSEMARY RAUGHTER

IRISH ACADEMIC PRESS
DUBLIN • PORTLAND, OR

First published in 2005 by
IRISH ACADEMIC PRESS
44, Northumberland Road, Dublin 4, Ireland

and in the United States of America by
IRISH ACADEMIC PRESS
c/o ISBS, Suite 300, 920 NE 58th Avenue
Portland, Oregon 97213–3644

WEBSITE: www.iap.ie

Copyright collection © 2005 Irish Academic Press
Copyright chapters © 2005 contributors

ISBN 0–7165–2759–6 (cloth)
ISBN 0–7165–2760–X (paper)

British Library Cataloguing in Publication Data
A catalogue entry is available on request

Library of Congress Cataloging-in-Publication Data
A catalog entry is available on request

Typeset by Carrigboy Typesetting Services, County Cork
Printed by in Great Britain by MPG Books Ltd, Bodmin, Cornwall

CONTENTS

FOREWORD

The writing and production of a book is always the result of a group process. The essays presented here are based on conference papers that mainly involved practioners of women's history who were also specialists in religious history drawn from different Christian traditions. Startlingly fresh and suggestive of further research, four of the essays provide case studies in historical recovery spanning eighteenth-century Catholic revival in post-Jacobite Ireland, Irish Presbyterian initiatives in evangelising parts of Asia, the activities of the Salvation Army in Ireland in the 1880's, and Irish nuns in nineteenth-century Chicago. Two essays examine the tools of historical method in reconstructing past lives and events. In the creative final essay a woman poet ponders the layered meanings of her nun-aunt's religious identity during a lifetime spent in the service of the sick.

The astonishing ability of women to re-invent themselves and cram adventures and enterprise into lives that appear outwardly staid is one of the suprises in store for the readers of the essays. As the practice of women's history widens to examine class, gender, ethnicity and race, the writing of women's religious experience will gain immeasurably in richness and analytical depth, advancing the frontiers opened up in this volume.

It is doubtful if the collection published here in book form by Irish Academic Press could have been edited without the tenacity and rigour of the editor, Rosemary Raughter, who had previously shown her mettle in the editing of the eighteenth-century section on 'Women and Religion' in *The Field Day Anthology of Irish Writing: Irish Women's Writings and Traditions,* Vol. 4 (Cork University Press, 2002). Both she and Irish Academic Press are to be congratulated on publishing the fine collection between the covers of this book.

MARGARET MACCURTAIN

ACKNOWLEDGEMENTS

The editor wishes to thank all the contributors for their patience and co-operation. In particular, Suellen Hoy provided assistance in the initial stages of this project, while Phil Kilroy's encouragement and friendship has been an essential support throughout.

A particular debt of gratitude is due to Margaret MacCurtain for her inspiration, interest and advice, and for her more than generous Foreword. Sister Pius of the South Presentation Convent, Cork, Sister Rosario of the Presentation Convent, George's Hill, Dublin and Patricia McLean of the Ulster Museum, Belfast were outstandingly helpful and courteous in locating illustrations. Thanks also to the Sisters of Mercy and the Sisters of the Good Shepherd, Chicago and to the Society of the Sacred Heart, Rome for permission to reproduce photographs, to the staff of the various libraries and archival institutions listed in the bibliography, to colleagues in the fields of women's history and women's studies and to Lisa Hyde of Irish Academic Press, who has guided this volume to completion.

Special thanks to friends and family for their encouragement, but a particular word of appreciation to John and Emma, who have been unfailingly supportive and tolerant of my preoccupation with the minutiae of past lives, and whose loving confidence has been a mainstay throughout.

LIST OF ILLUSTRATIONS

INTRODUCTION

Rosemary Raughter

This collection of essays had its origins in a conference hosted by the Women's Education, Research and Resource Centre (WERRC) at University College, Dublin which was attended by historians, researchers and post-graduate students, archivists of religious orders and faith-based institutions, and interested laypeople and members of a number of congregations and organisations. The topic, 'The writing of religious women's history', was suggested by Dr Margaret MacCurtain – herself a pioneering historian of women's history, with a particular interest in female spirituality and religious practice – and the objectives of the event were to provide a forum for those currently working in this field, both in Ireland and abroad, to assess the advances made in recent decades, to identify some of the resources available for research and to point the way to future lines of investigation.

While the contributions and the ensuing exchanges were wide-ranging, covering a broad span in chronological and geographical as well as in confessional terms, the primary fact emerging from the discussion – and consequently from the essays in this collection – was the dichotomy confronting any enquiry into the role of women in religion, and specifically in the various branches of Christianity over the two millennia of its existence. On the one hand, women were excluded from positions of authority and leadership, debarred from ordination, discouraged from speaking publicly, and subjected to an interpretation of the Scriptures which sanctioned their subservience in the private as in the public sphere. Thus, while St Paul asserted the unity of all believers in Christ and made reference to numerous women who participated in the ministry of the early church, he also reflected the culture and circumstances of his time in directives on wives' subjection to their husbands and on women's status in the church: they should, he wrote, 'learn in silence with due subjection . . . not to teach, nor to usurp authority over the man, but to be in silence.'[1] It was on teachings such as these that the most influential scholars of the

1

early church and of the medieval period based their own view of the female role, and the Reformation, while arguably enhancing women's status as wives and mothers and encouraging their access to education, maintained the male monopoly on ordination and church government.

There were, indeed, exceptions to this experience of subjugation and exclusion, and women's dissatisfaction with the options available to them may be inferred, for instance, from the female attraction to more radical versions of Protestantism which emerged in the post-Reformation period. While there were undoubtedly a number of factors behind this positive response, women clearly found in such groupings a degree of autonomy unavailable to them in mainstream denominations, and many certainly welcomed the opportunities for action and even for authority which these sects provided. These opportunities, however, rarely amounted to full equality – moreover, such independence as female adherents achieved invariably diminished with the passing of the initial missionary phase. Meanwhile, Catholic women responded to the spirit of the Counter-Reformation by demanding a more active apostolate, but were forced to modify their initiatives to conform to ecclesiastical officials' favoured model of the conventual life and of the female role and nature.[2]

Despite such setbacks, however, women throughout the period covered by this collection have found themselves impelled to activism by their faith. The impact of the evangelicalism which serves as the background to many of the essays which follow, is particularly instructive. At first sight, the evangelical legacy was a conservative one, promoting as it did the concept of separate spheres: thus, while men monopolized the public world, women were pre-eminent in the domestic arena, with responsibility for the education of children, the maintenance of Christian values in the home and the care of the sick and afflicted. At the same time, the very qualities – tenderness, patience, compassion – which supposedly fitted women for such a role endowed them with a moral superiority, which dignified their status and enhanced their sense of Christian mission. As one such woman, writing in 1839, argued

> By entrusting to woman a revelation of himself, God has pointed out whom he intends for his missionaries upon earth . . . Let men enjoy in peace and triumph the intellectual kingdom which is theirs, and which, doubtless, was intended for them; let us

participate in its privileges without desiring to share its domination. The moral world is ours – ours by position, ours by qualification, ours by the very indication of God himself, who has deigned to put in woman's heart the only feeling . . . which affords the faintest representation of his most unextinguishable love to us, his erring and strayed children.[3]

Such an interpretation, while validating prevailing views of the female role and nature, clearly carried much more radical implications, authorising women to extend their usefulness beyond their duties as wives and mothers to the spiritual and moral regeneration of society as a whole. Evangelical religion, therefore, was a vital incentive to the nineteenth-century female involvement in missionary, philanthropic, temperance, educational and reformist effort, which in turn fuelled awareness of women's impotence to effect reform and the demand for public and political equality.

These initiatives, then, provide telling evidence of the dichotomy mentioned earlier. Throughout the centuries, and in defiance of their secondary status in institutional religion, pious females have drawn from their faith not only spiritual sustenance and emotional support but justification for assertiveness and for initiative in very many areas of life: as Margaret MacCurtain has uncompromisingly stated, of the early modern and modern periods, 'for women of all classes . . . religion provided the most powerful incentive for experiencing autonomy and for independent action'.[4] The essays in *Religious Women and their History: Breaking the Silence* are united by this theme of opportunity, by the uses which women made of it in a variety of circumstances, and by the constraints on their scope for action. As historians of women have frequently noted, disruption of the existing order, whether social, political or religious, has tended to favour female enterprise, although advances made at such moments have almost invariably been undermined with the return of stability. In such a context, Rosemary Raughter shows, eighteenth-century Catholic women enjoyed a freedom which was to decline as Irish Catholicism emerged from the rigours of the penal period and as structures of ecclesiastical authority were re-established. Women such as Nano Nagle, Teresa Mulally and their associates were prompted to action by piety; they established a range of projects which benefitted the most needy and marginalized members of society, in promoting Catholic teaching, practice and values they made a major contribution to the Catholic revival of the late eighteenth century, and their vision of a socially-active sisterhood transformed the character of the female religious life in Ireland. They did all this, moreover, in the face not only of anti-Catholic legislation but of distrust from within their own community. The weakness of ecclesiastical structures in mid-eighteenth-century Ireland allowed laywomen like Nagle and Mulally some degree of freedom in the establishment and management of their projects. With the re-establishment of hierarchical authority that autonomy was sharply diminished and ultimately, in common with their co-religionists in Counter-Reformation Europe, charitable Catholic women accepted the restrictions inherent in membership of a religious congregation as the price to be paid for the survival of their projects and for continued permission to be active.

Women's involvement in faith-based philanthropy was, in fact, the primary means by which they achieved a place in the public arena, although few of those involved envisaged, much less sought, such an outcome. Phil Kilroy, biographer of Madeleine Sophie Barat, identifies Barat as a counter-revolutionary in political terms but a radical in her vision of educational opportunities for women. Born in 1779 in Burgundy, the young Sophie witnessed the effects of the French Revolution at first hand. In 1800 she founded the Society of the Sacred Heart, going on to establish a network of schools throughout Europe and America. As leader of the Society, she displayed impressive entre-preneurial skills, travelled extensively, negotiated with governments and with the papacy, and held a position of power and influence both in Catholic church circles and in wider society. By the time of her death in 1865, the society which she had founded had 3,359 members, with eighty-nine houses throughout the world. A private woman, Barat's life was lived in the public eye, and in extending the educational oppor-tunities available to girls, she was part of the movement which drew women out of the private and into the public domain, and was herself an outstanding example of this development. She had also negotiated a lengthy spiritual journey which took her from the severe and sin-obsessed religion of her youth to the concept of an approachable and loving God, as expressed in devotion to the Sacred Heart. In sum-marising Barat's relations with her church, Kilroy epitomises the dilemma faced by a number of other women whose experience is described in this volume. Sophie, she writes,

... was a deeply religious woman and her life was lived within the basic belief in the existence of God, revealed in Jesus Christ. For her, the Catholic Church was the church of Christ and she was faithful to its teaching, nourished by its sacraments and attentive to the demands it made of her . . . While she did not question any of the fundamental aspects of her faith-world, Sophie's needs and her own experience of life led her to question, to challenge and change what had been given to her as immutable.

While pursuing her own personal and inner journey, Barat was a product of her time and culture. Thus, the evangelicalism of the nineteenth century suffused all branches of Christianity, affecting both Protestantism and Catholicism with its message of spiritual regeneration and moral reform. A particularly noteworthy aspect of this in the Irish context was the proliferation of the female religious orders: in the course of the century the number of convents in Ireland grew from eleven to 368, with the number of nuns increasing eightfold between 1841 and 1901. From an early stage nuns shared in the common Irish experience of emigration, contributing to the development of social and educational services in their chosen areas of settlement. Suellen Hoy shows how Irish–American sisters initiated action in North America, embarking on their efforts while Chicago was still no more than 'a primitive western outpost' and the final destination of many thousands of destitute Irish immigrants. In these demanding circumstances, Irish Sisters of Mercy established schools, adult education classes, an employment bureau, a dispensary, orphanages, St Xavier Academy and Mercy Hospital, and by mid-century had established the kind of social settlement more usually associated with the work of late nineteenth-century feminist reformers like Jane Addams or Ellen Gates Starr. Nevertheless, Hoy argues, the work of these Mercy nuns, as of the Sisters of the Good Shepherd, who arrived in Chicago in 1859 and opened a magdalen asylum and an industrial school for girls, has been neglected by American historians of women in favour of the activities of middle-class Protestant reformers who did very similar work, but who went on – as nuns did not – to link the evils which they witnessed to the demands for women's rights.

While membership of a religious congregation was, by and large, a necessary pre-condition of Catholic women's public involvement,

Protestant women were free of the restrictions which this implied. Nevertheless, those who wished to have an active role in the religious sphere generally found themselves most effective in association with others of similar views. Certainly this is true of the female members of the Salvation Army who arrived in Belfast in 1880 under the command of Caroline Reynolds to preach the gospel to their target audience of the irreligious and the poor. Identified by Janice Holmes as primarily young, English, single and of 'respectable' working-class origin, these women quickly found themselves embroiled in political conflict and sectarian tensions of which they had little or no prior knowledge. In spite of this, they managed to pursue their mission with considerable success. As Holmes summarises their achievement:

> These were . . . more than just 'simple women'. Uneducated they may have been, and untrained in the skills of pulpit oratory, but between them they laid the foundation upon which an entire denomination was built. Unfortunately, the religious divisions within nineteenth-century Irish society overshadowed the magnitude of their achievement. The fact that it was women in charge of this religious effort – unusual behaviour by any standard – was virtually ignored in favour of the public order implications of their activity.

By the time Caroline Reynolds left Ireland in 1882, the number of Army women had risen from five to thirty-five, and fifteen Salvation Army corps, or congregations, had been established across Ulster. Again, however, the pattern of diminishing autonomy applied: with the institutionalisation of the Salvation Army in Ireland, women members were increasingly relegated to a supportive role within the movement which they had helped to establish.

Just as young women who joined the Salvation Army found themselves confronting, and meeting, challenges which they could scarcely have imagined, so too did those who answered the Presbyterian Zenana Mission's appeal for workers in India and China. Founded in 1874 with the aim of 'promoting Christianity among the women of the East', over the next thirty years the Mission sent a total of 101 missionary women abroad, and Myrtle Hill's analysis of its records reveals significant and sometimes unexpected factors underlying the motivation and experience of those involved. Hill notes the opportunities for both paid and voluntary employment offered by missionary work. Zenana missionaries received the most modern training available at the time, had excellent prospects of professional advancement and enjoyed a degree of independence which would have been impossible at home. For instance, at a time when medical training for women was still controversial and when women wishing to practice as doctors in Britain and Ireland faced considerable prejudice, female doctors were particularly in demand for work in the mission field. Meanwhile, the organisation's missionary efforts were dependent on a committed body of female support at home, and this involvement, while it could be regarded as traditionally feminine in being voluntary and supportive, also had the potential to expand women's sphere of interest and influence. As Hill argues,

> With women supporting each other through prayer meetings, sewing circles and fundraising, home mission work opened new possibilities for female assertion inside and outside the home. In a venture which took them out of the private sphere to become part of a more public campaign to reform the world, many of these women enhanced their personal standing in the family, the congregation and the wider religious culture in which they operated.

This collection builds on, and extends the remit of a body of work on Irish women's religious belief and practice which has appeared in the course of the past twenty-five years. The contributions to the groundbreaking collection *Women in Irish society*[5] included a number which identified the significance of faith and denominational affiliation in women's lives, and the extent to which academic scholarship had advanced in this area was apparent in Caitriona Clear's *Nuns in Nineteenth-Century Ireland*,[6] which subjected to rigorous examination and analysis a topic to which so much myth had attached over the years. The experience of female religious has since provided fertile ground for a number of other researchers, as has the powerful impact of evangelicalism on women and the female involvement in movements such as Quakerism, Methodism and the Ulster Revival of 1859, while historians of women's educational, temperance, philanthropic and reformist effort have explored the part played by religious feeling in this involvement.[7] One of the most significant and prolific contributors to this debate has been Maria Luddy who, as Director of the Women's History Project, oversaw the survey of 420 public and private repositories in the Republic of Ireland and in Northern Ireland for material relating to the history of women in Ireland from the earliest times to the present. *The Directory of Sources for the History of Women in Ireland*, which appeared in 1999, contains information on over 14,000 collections and sources in 262 repositories, among which were a large number of convent archives containing a wealth of information on Catholic female religious life in Ireland. In her essay Luddy explores the range of material available, and suggests its usefulness in uncovering not only the role of religion in women's lives over the past two hundred years but also to examine many aspects of social history over that period. She also discusses issues of access, and offers pointers to possibilities for future research, providing a reminder of the range of questions still remaining to be addressed in this area, as in the whole field of religious women's history.

The 'silence' referred to in the title of this collection applies to the subjection imposed on women over the centuries by institutional Christianity and its 'breaking' to the process of recovering the stories of those who existed within those structures and who found their own ways of subverting them. Eilean Ní Chuilleanain's poem and short essay on the use of language, and the gains as well as the surrenders which religious life entailed, suggest the complexities, the conflicts and, indeed, the surprises which await in the study of religious women's history. Ní Chuilleanain celebrates her memory of her aunt, Anna Cullinane – or Sister Mary Antony of the Franciscans of Calais – and in doing so recaptures the experience of so many Irishwomen of all denominations, whose commitment on behalf of their faith challenged their perceptions, distanced them from all that was familiar and extended the dimensions of their world. Mastering their environment, learning a language which expressed the new reality of their lives but which also preserved links with the outside world and with their own past, they left stories which have the potential to extend our knowledge of the past and of ourselves.

THE WRITING OF RELIGIOUS WOMEN'S HISTORY: MADELEINE SOPHIE BARAT (1779–1865)[1]

Phil Kilroy

> For she had had a great variety of selves to call upon, far more than we have been able to find room for, since a biography is considered complete if it merely accounts for six or seven selves, whereas a person may well have as many thousand.
>
> Virginia Woolf, *Orlando*[2]

> Let any woman imagine for a moment a biography of herself based on those records she has left, those memories fresh in the minds of surviving friends, those letters that chanced to be kept, those impressions made, perhaps, on the biographer who was casually met in the subject's later years. What secrets, what virtues, what passions, what discipline, what quarrels would, on the subject's death, be lost forever? How much would have vanished or been distorted or changed, even in our memories? We tell ourselves stories of our past, make fictions or stories of it, and these narrations *become* the past, the only part of our lives that is not submerged.
>
> Carolyn G. Heilbrun, *Writing a Woman's life*[3]

Both Virginia Woolf and Carolyn Heilbrun express reservations about the use and validity of biography when presenting a life. The self is far too rich and complex a reality to be defined and confined by biography. Besides, the biographer chooses how to present her subject, and reads the documentation in the light of her own consciousness and interests. For example, both Adèle Cahier and Louis Baunard were invited to write lives of Sophie Barat in the late nineteenth century.[4] The commission given to Baunard was specifically in view of the canonisation process that had begun in 1879, soon after

Sophie's death. The purpose was to present her as a holy woman, worthy of sainthood, thus ensuring that her actual life and legacy were interpreted in the light of this ultimate aim.

Yet in any age biography has an objective and purpose. There is always an agenda, an interest, a perspective, and the genre of biography is as revisionist as any other form of history. The most recent biography[5] was commissioned to celebrate the 200 years of the existence of the Society of the Sacred Heart, founded by Sophie Barat in 1800. It has another agenda, different from that which faced Cahier and Baunard. Because of that, and because the archives and documents consulted are far more easily accessible today than in the late nineteenth century, this biography reflects the use of sources not available, particularly, to Adèle Cahier who, as a member of the Society of the Sacred Heart, was constrained in the sources outside the congregation to which she had access. This new biography is a study of Sophie Barat's life before her death in 1865, before the process of canonisation had begun, and it is written from within the perspective of women's history. Yet while it is a substantial statement about Sophie, it can never be definitive. There is always more to learn, to discover, to understand. By way of helping this process, I would like to discuss four aspects of Sophie Barat's life: the formative nature of her early life; her place among other women in her time; her development of leadership; and her capacity to tell the stories of the Society's foundation.

FORMATIVE NATURE OF HER EARLY LIFE

The story of Sophie Barat's life begins in 1779 in the little Burgundian town of Joigny, where she was born late in the evening of 12 December, while a fire raged outside her home in the rue du Puits Chardon. Her mother, Madeleine Foufée, was so distressed by the fire that she gave birth two months prematurely. While Jacques Barat and his daughter, Marie-Louise, looked after Madame Barat, Sophie's elder brother, Louis, took his little sister to the church nearby to have her baptised. She was frail and in danger of death, but she survived and gradually strengthened. The image of fire characterised Sophie personally and also the many revolutions and intense experiences that she confronted in the course of her long life.

At the time of Sophie's childhood in Joigny the spirit of the Enlightenment was gradually permeating the consciousness of European society, insisting that human beings, endowed with rational capacities, could succeed in making sense of their lives, indeed transform them into works of art. Part of this consciousness was a new spirit of optimism, as well as a critique of the institutions of society, especially the church. The anti-clerical stance, among the French *philosophes* in particular, came at a time when the Catholic Church itself had undergone radical change. Although it had reformed itself successfully in accordance with the decrees of the Council of Trent, in the wake of the Reformation it had become a church closed in upon itself, distrustful of life and of the world, focusing on the authority of the bishops and clergy, and on the reform of clerical training and the care of parishes. It became elitist, frowning on local, popular expressions of Catholicism and discouraging many of the practices of popular religion. This Tridentine church in France was marked by Jansenism, a further reform movement rooted in the theology of predestination. As a result of this influence, by the late eighteenth century Catholics in France were weighed down by an image of God that was severe, threatening and demanding, and by the conviction that human nature was profoundly sinful, that human beings were incapable of carrying out any good act. The mediation of the clergy was seen as the only hope of bridging the gap between God and the sinner. It was considered almost impossible to make a good confession and communion, such was the sinfulness of the human being. The impact of this devastating view of human nature meant that the practice of approaching God in sacrament had diminished, especially among the male members of the population.[6]

The region of the Yonne was considered to be among the most Jansenistic in France, and as a child and young adult in Joigny Sophie imbibed these varying strands of religious thinking and practice. In addition, her childhood experiences were bound up with those of France itself on the eve of the Revolution. Her adolescence was marked by the unrest and turbulence of 1789, by the fall of the monarchy, and by the Terror, and the memory of these events stayed with her throughout her life. She went on to live through the reign of Napoleon, the restoration of the Bourbons, the July Revolution of 1830 and the revolutions of 1848. The impact of the French Revolution reverberated throughout the nineteenth century, and

Sophie's own journey was undertaken against a background of further unrest, further revolution and further change. Yet she herself was not revolutionary in the political sense, but rather counter-revolutionary, since her experience of the Revolution, especially of the Terror in Joigny and Paris, made her fearful of the extremes of revolutionary energy. Her abiding instinct, expressed in her relationships and in her understanding of institutions, was to conserve, to restore, to repair, to renew.

SOPHIE BARAT'S PLACE AMONG OTHER WOMEN OF HER TIME

Sophie was living in Paris when the revolutionary period gave way to the rise of Napoleon and the establishment of the Empire. At this time, in a bid to restore the primacy of religion and the place of the church, many women all over France initiated small communities focused on social work, mostly in education and health.[7] These projects began in towns, villages and cities, and gradually mushroomed throughout France and Europe, and into the wider world. Sophie Barat was part of that impulse and energy. Between 1800 and 1820 thirty-five new communities of women, including the Society of the Sacred Heart, were founded in France; and each year between 1820 and 1880 six new communities were founded. The founders of these communities came from all sections of French society, and included fifty-three from the lower bourgeoisie, among them Sophie Barat herself.[8]

Sophie's leadership of the Society of the Sacred Heart was facilitated by the education she had received as a child and teenager, and by her gift for making friendships. In Joigny her elder brother, Louis, decided to become her tutor and teach her all that he had learned, first as a boy at the Collège St Jacques in Joigny and then at the seminary at Sens, where he studied for the priesthood. When he moved to Paris in 1795 he persuaded his parents to allow Sophie to join him there and continue her education. This formation of Sophie was austere, severe and demanding, and, while she gained a great deal in terms of a basic education and a certain extension of learning, she paid the price in permanent damage to her health. In relation to her life's work, the educational preparation provided by Louis was crucial for Sophie's leadership of the Society of the Sacred Heart. It provided her with an ascendancy over her colleagues, most of whom had been born into aristocratic and upper bourgeois French families.

1. Signature of Sophie Barat as a young woman, Sophie Barat to Adrienne Michel, Grenoble, 11 August 1810. (General Archives, Society of the Sacred Heart, Rome).

In addition, Sophie had a gift for making friendships, which even Louis's influence could not suppress, and she exercised her leadership, especially in the early years, through the personal relationships that she created with her colleagues. She was surrounded by gifted and energetic women, and consciously used her education and her capacity to relate to maintain her position as the elected superior general of the communities.

SOPHIE BARAT'S DEVELOPMENT OF LEADERSHIP

By fulfilling her role in the Society of the Sacred Heart Sophie Barat opened up new paths for women. Indeed, she and the numerous other women who established new congregations of women in France in the early nineteenth century were welcomed and valued by clerics because they were desperately needed within the church. Long before the Revolution women outnumbered men as worshippers and as active participants in parish life. So, while the value of women in themselves, their rights and dignity, were not recognised in the Declaration of the Rights of Man (1789), in the church women were seen as the way to bring men back to the practice of the faith. In that respect and for that purpose, women were useful and necessary, and that need opened a space for the initiatives of women such as Sophie Barat. The market for education and health care was immense, and between them these women carved out certain areas in which to work, and displayed great entrepreneurial skills in maintaining and extending their communities. Sophie Barat's chosen field of activity was the education of young women of the aristocracy and upper middle class, and the education of the poor, and to this purpose she established boarding schools and poor schools, usually on the same property. By the time of her death in 1865 she presided over an international community of 3,359 women, who were inspired by a spiritual ideal and offered a service of education in Europe, North Africa, and North and South America.

In the course of her life Sophie bought and sold large schools and properties. She handled intricate finances deftly, and made astute deals and decisions. A woman of great entrepreneurial skills, she enjoyed buying and selling, although she abhorred debts of any kind – even in the last weeks of her life she ensured that her nephew, Stanislas, repaid her a small sum of money that he had borrowed. Most of her business affairs were carried out through the medium of her letters, which cover a range of subjects and show Sophie at work as a leader, friend, guide and businesswoman all in one. Through her letter-writing Sophie discovered her personal style of leadership and gradually found how to articulate it. She used a rhetoric in conversation and letter-writing that suited the demands of her leadership.[9] This enabled her to overcome obstacles and pursue her goals in a world where female leadership was greeted with suspicion and often with outright hostility. With the benefit of our consciousness today, we can grasp what Sophie Barat was straining after in her day. She did not have the words, the social constructs or the general acknowledgement of the issue of women in society that have come to the fore

2. Gardens of the Hotel Biron, rue de Varenne, Paris (now the Rodin Museum), bought by Sophie Barat in 1820 as headquarters of the Society of the Sacred Heart. (General Archives, Society of the Sacred Heart, Rome).

in our time. Without such social confirmation and assurance, Sophie Barat made her way with her colleagues in the Society of the Sacred Heart, with church and with government bodies, in Paris, in Rome and throughout the areas where the Society was active during her lifetime.

This was a real achievement because, like all women of her time, Sophie was affected by the low image that women had in society generally. Thus, Edme Davier, one of Joigny's most notable citizens and the founder of the school where her brother was educated, stated that:

> A woman is a spoilt creature who changes appearance and character just as she wishes. She is dishonest in her thoughts, scheming in her emotions, calculating in her views, flighty in her conversations, coquettish in her manners. She has affected airs, is deceitful about her virtues, self-interested in her generosity,

and hypocritical about her economies. She is always crafty, always ambiguous and always telling lies. Now that, more or less, is what women are like.[10]

The view of women as secondary and inferior to men was deeply embedded in the consciousness of men and women. In the realm of religion it was couched in theological language and internalised in the life of prayer and the practice of faith. The *philosophes* of the Enlightenment, whose rational spirit critiqued the institutions of church and state, did not promote the equality or the rights of women, or indeed the equality and rights of the servant and non-propertied classes. Rather they continued to presume that men (white, wealthy and educated) were the norm, and they measured women against this assumption.[11] The radical thinkers and activists of the Revolution, with the notable exception of Condorcet, concurred with this judgement. Women who had hoped for inclusion in the revolutionary spirit found they had been useful only for a time, a common experience of women in any revolutionary period.[12] Negative views of women were further reinforced by Napoleon, whose Civil Code defined the limited rights and extensive duties of women for the nineteenth century, imposing rigid legal subordination on women in the family and in the state.[13]

In this context Sophie Barat's leadership of the Society of the Sacred Heart was remarkable, and often more for her actions than for her rhetoric. While Sophie retained the language of conformity, she moved as she needed to meet the requirements of the moment. In a world where woman's powers and skills were not readily recognised or valued by either men or women, Sophie Barat found her way within constrictions and achieved her goals. In that sense she was the supreme diplomat, forced to use a certain type of language to make herself understood. She had no script to follow and few models to learn from, and she was often compelled to work on her own. She prepared the way for a new space and place for women far beyond her own time. Gerda Lerner, explaining the criteria for inclusion in her study of the creation of feminist consciousness, notes:

I have included many women who would not have defined themselves as feminist in their own time, even allowing for the fact that the word itself did not appear until late in the nineteenth century. Such women would have denied that they were concerned with problems of women as such and several of them were explicitly opposed to women's rights movements. I have included some of them, such as female mystics or early proponents of women's education, because their work and thought directly contributed to the development of feminist consciousness, whether they so intended or not.[14]

That, in a sense, was the public narrative of Sophie Barat, the role presentation of a superior general at the centre of a new group of women, involved in education in France, Europe, Africa and the Americas. As a nineteenth-century woman Sophie Barat found her way out of a private life into a public role with a public profile, and she did this because she, with her colleagues, had a service to offer that met a need in society and in the church. However, another inner narrative was taking place at the same time, one that informed the outer, and gave the impulse and energy to sustain so much activity. While she was engaged in the founding and consolidation of the Society of the Sacred Heart, Sophie made a spiritual journey, in the course of which she continually strove to transform the image of a severe, harsh and Jansensist God into one of warmth, love and vulnerability. Although her outer success was the focus of her fame in the nineteenth century and beyond, her inner achievement had greater, longer-term consequences for the image of the divine, of the holy, in our time.

Sophie was endowed with a remarkable capacity for human relationships and she used that gift to good effect in her leadership of the Society of the Sacred Heart. Yet it took great and continual efforts throughout her life to face her own self-image, her image of God, her shadow self and the shadow self of her colleagues. On the one hand the image of God could be cold, empty, harsh, critical and emotionally frozen. On the other hand it could be warm, full of energy, gentle, generous-minded and vulnerable. It was never easy, and it demanded all her courage to trust enough to let go of old certainties, old burdens. In her testament to the Society of the Sacred Heart, read after her death, Sophie Barat admitted she had only realised a part of what she had searched for all her life and that her journey was not over, nor was that of the Society.

Sophie Barat was a deeply religious woman and her life was lived within the basic belief in the existence of God, revealed in Jesus

Christ. For her the Catholic Church was the church of Christ, and she was faithful to its teaching, nourished by its sacraments and attentive to the demands it made of her as superior general of the Society of the Sacred Heart. She loved and practised many devotions that stemmed from either medieval France or the ultramontane movement of the nineteenth century.[15] While she did not question any of the fundamental aspects of her faith-world, Sophie's needs and her own experience of life led her to question, to challenge and to change what had been given to her as immutable. She felt secure in her beliefs and practices, and within those she created new and different spaces for women, and she expanded the scope of her own authority and freedom of action in a way that few questioned, especially in the later years of her life, by which time she had become a legend.

SOPHIE BARAT'S CAPACITY TO TELL THE STORIES
OF THE SOCIETY'S FOUNDATION

At the beginning of her religious life Sophie was presented with a story, told her by Joseph Varin, that placed her in contact with influences and movements current within France, the Austrian Empire and Italy.[16] Through these she was introduced to several people whose lives and narratives would affect her profoundly. In later years these months were the subject of recall and the focus of many stories, told by herself and others, that became a way of relating the origins of the Society of the Sacred Heart. They became the founding myth and the source of inspiration when new members wanted to discover how the Society had been initiated. There is energy and idealism in the stories, rooted in the difficult reality of the French Revolution. There is also a sense of empowerment, which generated new hopes and possibilities for the future. The stories and their narrators captured the imagination of women, from all walks of life and many different backgrounds, who wanted to do something with their lives and to counteract the horrors of war and destruction. Since almost the whole of Sophie's life was marked by war or revolution, these stories of the origins of the Society of the Sacred Heart were told many times, with the retelling retaining the central vision and initiative, born in a time of distress and upheaval. The retelling, of course, had a clarity and definition that only a backward view of the actual events could grasp, and some difficult elements in the stories were 'forgotten' or glossed over in the effort to keep the central core intact and preserve the myth.

When Sophie met Joseph Varin, in Paris in 1800, he told her about his former colleague, Léonor de Tournély, who as a young priest had founded an association of priests called the Society of the Sacred Heart, committed to the restoration of the Jesuits in France. Varin himself had joined the Society in 1794 and, with others, followed de Tournély through warring Europe before finally settling at Hegenbrunn near Vienna. There the little group lived an austere life, rather more in keeping with the life of Trappist monks than that of Jesuits in waiting. Indeed, at this time they saw themselves essentially as contemplatives, leaving their solitude only to minister in surrounding parishes. Like other such communities scattered throughout Europe at this time, they drew energy and support from one another, and set up a network that enabled them to survive the profound upheavals of the period.[17]

In January 1796 de Tournély decided to found an association of women, also called the Society of the Sacred Heart. Like the male association, its inspiration would be drawn from the Jesuit rule, but it would be applied in accordance with the place of women in the church, particularly their non-clerical status.[18] De Tournély's concept was very far from that of the Englishwoman Mary Ward who, in the seventeenth century, had sought to establish an active form of religious life for women, based on the Jesuit rule and free of the solemn vows that imposed strict papal cloistering. However, Ward's radical vision – which encompassed greater freedom of movement for women religious, reflecting a closer, simpler relationship to society in general – was unthinkable in the church of the seventeenth century, as it continued to be in that of the eighteenth century.[19] Certainly, de Tournély envisaged the women of his association as contemplatives, who would be cloistered in accordance with the customs of religious life before the Revolution, while also being involved in education and nursing.[20]

In fact, de Tournély's project of a women's association was not realised during his lifetime, and he himself died in July 1797. Following his death the Fathers of the Sacred Heart became absorbed into another association, the Fathers of the Faith, founded by Nicholas Paccanari. This had a women's branch, called the Dilette de Gesù (Beloved of Jesus), which Sophie Barat entered in Paris in 1800. Yet de Tournély's initial impulse was not lost and, although muted for a time, it re-emerged some years later in France, through Sophie Barat.[21]

While Sophie had heard de Tournély's story and told it herself down the years, she went on to create her own story and myth, and merged the two in her own way. She did not articulate her own story immediately, but she found and lived it long before she spoke about it. The Society of the Sacred Heart was to be born in an inner world and be nourished from an inner place. For Sophie Barat the Society was to be a centre of prayer and inner spiritual work, effective in ways not readily perceived. This aspect and dimension was to inform and nourish all that the Society would do in the field of education. Many years later Sophie spoke about these early years. She outlined the original impulse, rooted in her experience of the Revolution:

> The first idea of the Society that we had . . . was to gather as many as possible of the true adorers of the Heart of Jesus in the Eucharist . . . At the end of the Terror and of the abominations of the Revolution against religion and the Blessed Sacrament . . . all hearts vibrated together in unison: Make reparation to Jesus Christ in the Blessed Sacrament . . . was the rallying cry . . . No two pious people meeting together would talk without trying to find some means of bringing Jesus Christ back into family life. . . .
>
> My original idea of our little Society of the Sacred Heart was to gather young girls together and establish *a little community that night and day would adore the Heart of Jesus, whose love had been desecrated in the Eucharist.* But I said to myself, when we are twenty-four religious, able to replace one another on a *prie-Dieu* for perpetual adoration, that will be something, and yet little enough for such a noble goal. . . . If we had *young pupils* whom we formed in the spirit of adoration and reparation, now that would be different! And I saw hundreds, thousands of adorers before a *perfect, universal monstrance, raised above the Church.*[22]
>
> 'That is it' I said to myself, as I was praying before a lonely tabernacle: 'we must dedicate ourselves to the education of youth, renew in souls the solid foundations of a living faith in the . . . Blessed Sacrament; [and] there fight the traces of Jansenism, which had led to [such] impiety. With the revelations of Jesus Christ to Blessed Margaret Mary concerning the devotion of reparation . . . to the Heart of Jesus in the Blessed Sacrament, we will raise

up a multitude of adorers from all the nations, to the very ends of the Earth.'[23]

This was a visionary insight, a development of de Tournély's original impulse, but based on Sophie's own response to the Revolution and the Terror. With her companions Sophie felt the need to renew a society that had become brutalized and violent, both in its sense of God and in its respect for human life. Over the years this intuition matured, developed and expanded into seeing education as the means and the way to renew society. Sophie always returned to that initial hope and desire to heal and renew society in France after the ravages of the revolution.

Sophie's development of de Tournély's idea was linked with her leadership of the Society of the Sacred Heart, and her intuition was confirmed by another story that she heard later and in which she herself was a central figure. In October 1807 a woman named Suzanne Geoffroy applied to become a member of the community that had recently been established in Poitiers and, as was the practice when the community met to relax, she recounted her life story to fellow members.[24] Suzanne Geoffroy was born in 1761 in the village of Tellié, in the diocese of Poitiers. The oldest of nine children, she had been brought up by a childless aunt and uncle. She was a vivacious child who found it hard to concentrate on her studies, despite having a tutor at home. As a young woman she was attracted to the Carmelites in Poitiers and in 1787 asked to join the community there. However, the prioress felt that Suzanne was not called to their life and advised her to speak to her Jesuit confessor, Father Drouard, who advised her to be patient.[25] When she pressed him to be more explicit he told her that in time she would enter an order that, while founded in Germany, would later be brought into France by someone who in 1787 was still a little girl: 'she who is destined to be the founder of this congregation in France is still playing with her dolls'.[26] Drouard explained that he received this prophecy from another Jesuit, Father Nectoux, who had been his teacher in Poitiers before the suppression of the Jesuits, and who had also foretold the horrors of the French Revolution, the growth of the counter-revolutionary movement and the triumph of religion (through the return of the Bourbons), all in highly apocalyptic terms. He described the future association of women in some detail, saying that it would be devoted to the Sacred Heart, modelled on the Jesuits, and characterised by gentleness and humility. Suzanne Geoffroy did not meet Sophie Barat until 1807, when she asked to join the newly formed Association of which Sophie was superior general, at that time called the Dames de l'Instruction Chrétienne. Her arrival and the stories she told certainly affected Sophie deeply. However, in the autumn of 1800, when Sophie met Joseph Varin for the first time, she knew nothing about these predictions of the Society of the Sacred Heart and of her future role in it. At this period there was no question of Sophie initiating a group of women for a particular work – in fact, she understood that she was entering an order already established in Italy, the Dilette di Gesù.

So in 1800 Sophie was told of Léonor de Tournély's intuitions and on that basis created a story of her own, which had its own narrative and text. In the course of her long period of leadership of the Society of the Sacred Heart, her understanding of this story was tested and refined. Others inside and outside the Society had different stories, narratives and texts, which were sometimes quite opposed to what Sophie saw as essential to the Society. Further, throughout Sophie's lifetime there were sub-stories, sub-narratives, sub-texts, which Sophie often did not know about and encountered only (if at all) in a time of crisis. She journeyed with both strands of narrative, and it took fifty years for her leadership role to be accepted and established. By 1851 the Society had come of age and then Sophie tried to provide the kind of structures that would enable it to continue when she had died.

In the course of her long life Sophie Barat was shaped and enriched by the interaction of her personal, inner journey, her network of relationships, and the spiritual ideals that motivated her and her friends. These three elements informed, modified and transformed Sophie Barat, and she emerged from this crucible of formation as a pioneer who, in the company of many gifted companions, forged her own style of leadership. When she died, at 85 years of age, sixty-three of them had been spent in leadership. Hers was a life lived constantly in the public eye, in the presence of her colleagues and a wider circle of friends, family and business contacts. Expectations that friends and colleagues placed on her were often hard to carry. While in her early years she strove to be perfect, in later life Sophie recognised that she was not a flawless leader. She thus recognised some of her limitations, but was blind to others. Some things she understood well, others she did not. Sophie Barat was a product of her time and culture, and she

3. Signature of Sophie Barat in old age, Sophie Barat to Anna du Rousier, Paris, 26 July 1864. (General Archives, Society of the Sacred Heart, Rome).

was affected by the circumstances that impelled her to shape the Society of the Sacred Heart. She had her own inner journey to make in life, with daunting hurdles and challenges. Few knew of these and what they cost Sophie. Her personal journey was a hidden narrative that profoundly affected the public story and myth around her.

At different stages in the course of her life Sophie took many steps forward alone. She found the courage to move out from the shadows of diffidence and to assume leadership. She used her unusual capacity for relationships and she inspired her companions. She learned the joy and pain of deep friendship, and the cost of possessiveness. She experienced rejection and ridicule from some of her closest companions, and from some sections of society and of the church. In the course of it all she found inner freedom and strength as an individual, and demonstrated the impact of power exercised with reticence. Each stage of the journey brought its pain and its joy, because her heart and courage were great enough to respond to life, even if at times she could barely imagine surviving another day. She found her source of strength in her faith in God and in the life of prayer that empowered her. That too was bought at a price, for she drew energy from a God mediated through the image of the Heart of Christ wounded on Calvary. This meant undoing the Jansenist image of God, not just for a time or during a phase in her life, but forever. Sophie Barat had an impulsive, energetic nature and it was that nature, that energy, that saw the Society through so many critical phases and that, in the end, ensured that it would not disintegrate. Sophie kept faith and saw her work through to the end. Yet she functioned best in her role and found her relationships through her leadership of the Society of the Sacred Heart. Few glimpsed the private, reticent Sophie Barat behind the role and there, in that private space, she searched and came to terms with herself, and made sense of her life. She struggled and came to terms with her own self, and she learnt painfully how to stand alone, in her own individuality. This was a unique achievement and yet a task that all face, in any age.

PIOUS OCCUPATIONS: FEMALE ACTIVISM AND THE CATHOLIC REVIVAL IN EIGHTEENTH-CENTURY IRELAND

Rosemary Raughter

I . . . should not have so long deferred the acknowledging your kind favour and telling you the pleasure it gave me to hear that [your] health was better. I hope it's so well restored that you . . . are able to go on with all your pious occupations as heretofore, with the spirit of zeal which the Almighty has, I think, given such a blessing to and success, as to have the schools so useful to such a number of poor children. And I hope the increase of the charities you get will enable you to daily add to the good you do . . . You may rely on us that every assistance in our power we shall give towards having an establishment of this Society in the metropolis . . . the good they would do would be more universally known and extend them in other parts of the Kingdom.[1]

Through the 'pious occupations' in which they engaged and the 'spirit of zeal' that inspired them, the author of this letter, Nano Nagle, and its recipient, Teresa Mulally, played a pivotal role in the Catholic revival in Ireland of the final decades of the eighteenth century. Together with numbers of other similarly motivated women, they set in hand a variety of projects, which addressed the evils of poverty and ignorance, promoted religion and morality, and laid the basis for the much more intensive initiatives of the next century. They did so as committed members of a church that, having weathered the most repressive phase of the penal legislation, was gradually re-establishing its structures and consolidating its position. This essay discusses the

25

role played by this female philanthropy in the Catholic resurgence, the factors that prompted it and permitted it to flourish, and the process whereby the relative independence of this period was curtailed, forcing charitable Catholic women to conform to ecclesiastical direction, and limiting their freedom of decision-making and of action.

The impulse that prompted Nagle, Mulally and their associates to action was shared by women throughout Catholic Europe in the century and a half following the Council of Trent. As Counter-Reformation influences penetrated western Catholicism, women's commitment to the Tridentine spirit was evident, not only in their fidelity to the doctrines and practices of religion, but also in their membership of a variety of new devotional and charitable associations. Most controversially, women's zeal for the faith led them to claim a more active apostolate than that approved by the ecclesiastical authorities. Thus, the organisations established by innovators such as Angela Merici, Mary Ward or Jeanne de Chantal, while demonstrating women's usefulness in furthering the interests of the faith, also aroused concern and distrust, and their subsequent histories demonstrate the institutional church's determination to ensure that the structures through which women operated should be canonically controlled, and that women's activity should not deviate from prevailing perceptions of the female role and nature.[2]

As Tridentine influences infiltrated Irish Catholicism in the course of the seventeenth and eighteenth centuries, Irish women reacted to them largely as their counterparts elsewhere in Europe had done. Their experience, however, was also a distinctive one. By 1750 official repression was largely a thing of the past, but it left Irish Catholicism with a legacy of internal disorganisation, institutional poverty and a habit of deference towards the political authorities, which was only gradually overcome.[3] Inevitably these factors impinged on Irish women's charitable and educational projects, and, as will be seen, the provisions of the penal legislation did affect both their approach to their work and attitudes towards it. At the same time it is possible to see this period as one of relative freedom for women within a church whose lines of authority had been weakened by decades of disruption. In such circumstances Irish ecclesiastics lacked the means, or indeed the will, to exert control over the initiatives of their more assertive female members, whose work they recognised in any case as an essential element in the project of religious regeneration in which they

4. Copy of Charles Turner's engraving of Nano Nagle in the British Museum. (Courtesy of the Presentation Sisters, South Presentation Convent, Cork).

themselves were engaged. This relative independence combined with the home-centred pattern of religious practice that was also a result of the penal legislation to create a 'matriarchal era' in Irish Catholicism, within which women had a vital role to play in the preservation and transmission of the faith, and a degree of female initiative was tolerated and indeed encouraged as a means to that end.[4]

However, while specific factors favoured Catholic women's participation in charity work during the second half of the eighteenth century, their activity was also part of a wider movement involving members of all religious denominations.[5] While virtually all practitioners claimed the Christian injunction to charity as their primary motivation, women's philanthropy also received sanction from the view that they were inherently equipped for such activity. Thus, Sarah Trimmer cited 'the tenderness which is allowed to be natural to our sex' as its principal qualification for charitable activity, while the Society for Promoting the Comforts of the Poor addressed its appeal for funds to 'ladies in the middle ranks of life' on the grounds that 'they have the most humane dispositions, and a lively feeling for the distresses of the poor'.[6] At the same time philanthropy used expertise acquired by women in the course of their daily lives. The skills involved in the management of a household, in childrearing, and in the care of the sick and old were as relevant to the philanthropic as to the domestic sphere, while women had commonly taken a leading part in the exercise of hospitality and benevolence within local communities. As daughters of a Catholic gentry family Nano and her sister Ann Nagle visited and assisted the poor in their neighbourhood, and Nano was directly inspired to begin her missionary enterprises by the 'idleness, dishonesty, impiety, drunkenness' that she encountered during such visits.[7] Similarly the pioneering educationalist Teresa Mulally remembered her mother distributing food to the needy of the locality during the very severe winter of 1739–40 and, as an adult herself, she followed this example: she 'made ointments and other medicines for the poor, and dressed their sores; and [she] was always, while able, attentive to her sick friends and neighbours'.[8]

Informal benevolence of this type assumed a new dimension in the course of the eighteenth century with the development of associated and organised philanthropy. Urbanisation gave greater visibility to the ever-present problem of distress, with the rural poor gravitating towards the towns, and especially towards Dublin, in search of food

5. Portrait of Nano Nagle, South Presentation Convent, Cork, having the same format as the engraving by Turner. (Courtesy of the Presentation Sisters, South Presentation Convent, Cork).

and work. This influx intensified pressure on the scant resources available to the local poor and prompted a response, part humanitarian and part pragmatic, from the propertied classes. The resulting expansion of organised philanthropy was limited in the short term. Most eighteenth-century charities were small in scale, precariously dependent on the generosity of the public and concentrated in larger urban areas. In the longer term, however, the movement involved growing numbers of women, both as activists and supporters, addressed itself to previously disregarded areas of need, and laid the basis for the much more systematic and widespread philanthropy of the next century.[9]

One of the principal characteristics of female philanthropy was its particular concern for needy women and children, and favourite objects of charity included orphans and poor children, elderly women, and homeless and unemployed girls. Nagle was one of the pioneers in this area, opening her first poor school in Cork in about 1755. By 1769 she had seven schools in the city, two for boys and five for girls, as well as a number of other projects, such as sick visiting, poor relief and missionary work, and an almshouse 'where poor old women may spin out their last thread'.[10] At about the same time Teresa Mulally was engaging in similar work in Dublin, where she founded the city's first Catholic charity school for girls in Mary's Lane in 1766. Becoming aware of the need for some provision for orphaned and homeless girls, Mulally subsequently established a boarding school, which expanded from five inmates at its opening in 1771 to twenty in 1783.[11]

Catholic women also became involved at an early stage in the area of rescue work. Nagle, possibly inspired by the example of Lady Arbella Denny's magdalen asylum, opened in Dublin in 1767, had planned to provide a similar shelter in Cork as 'a receptacle for those unhappy females, who, tired in the ways of shame and iniquity, would return to God by repentance; if they had only a place to receive them'.[12] However, she died before she could carry out this intention. The first Catholic institution of this kind was founded in Townsend Street, Dublin, in 1797 by Bridget Burke. Shocked by an encounter with a prostitute, Burke embarked on a campaign 'to reclaim fallen women' by 'inducing them to leave the habitations of sin, and procuring respectable lodgings for them'. By 1821 her institution had thirty-seven residents, employed, as a contemporary account described it, 'in the more laborious occupations of female industry', such as laundry work and needlework.[13]

A notable feature of all these initiatives, and of women's philanthropy in general, was their reliance on female patronage and support. Thus, Teresa Mulally, in an 'Address to the Charitable of St Michan's Parish', pleaded the pressing need for instruction of 'poor children of the female sex', argued the 'peculiar abilities' of women to supply it and, in appealing for support for the scheme, addressed herself generally to 'the charity of the faithful', but especially to 'the ladies, whose usual tenderness for the poor in general cannot but show a particular feeling for the distressed members of their own sex'.[14] The records of her institution demonstrate the generosity of women's response to such appeals: of the eighty-four individuals who subscribed over the period 1766–72, sixty-five were female, and when Mulally sought funds to establish a convent at George's Hill some years later ten of the eighteen donors were women. One of the first and most generous of Mulally's benefactors was Mrs Coppinger, a member of the Bellew family, who donated twenty pounds towards the upkeep of the school and was invited to become president of the charity. Mrs Coppinger also supported the convent fund, heading the list with 'a donation of thousands'. Other sizeable contributions came from Mrs Fay, who subscribed 296 pounds, and Mrs Comerford, Miss Nevin and Mrs Shee, each of whom gave one hundred pounds. Like other contemporary charities, Mulally's school depended in part on the proceeds of the labour of its inmates, and again female supporters figured prominently in this source of income, with ladies such as Lady Fingall and female members of the Bellew family being among the chief customers for articles such as lace, gloves or other needlework produced by the children.[15]

In establishing her charities Mulally applied for assistance to 'some of the high Catholic families of the kingdom'. The records of her institution reveal her chief supporters to have been either ladies of the Catholic aristocracy and gentry, such as Mrs Coppinger, Lady Fingall or Mrs Talbot of Malahide, or the wives and daughters of the urban mercantile elite. Mulally's own father had been a merchant, while Miss Ann Corballis and Miss Judith Clinch, both of whom were associated with her in the running of her school, belonged to prominent Dublin trading families.[16] Nagle, too, received substantial backing for her charitable ventures from the Catholic gentry and mercantile classes, to which she herself had connections. Through her mother, Ann Mathew, and her father, Garret Nagle, she was descended from

6. Presentation convent and school, George's Hill, Dublin, built by Teresa Mulally. The building was completed in 1789, and the Presentation Sisters were established there in 1794. This photograph dates from the late nineteenth or early twentieth century. (Courtesy of the Presentation Sisters, George's Hill, Dublin).

two of the leading Catholic families in Munster, while her uncle, Joseph Nagle, a lawyer and entrepreneur, was one of the wealthiest Catholics in Cork and Nano's most significant benefactor.[17] Most of her earliest associates came from a similar background. Of the first Irish Ursulines, for instance, Eleanor Fitzsimon's father was a Dublin merchant, Margaret Nagle was the daughter of David Nagle of Cork, who was engaged in the victualling trade, and Elizabeth Coppinger and her cousin, Mary Kavanagh, belonged to prominent Catholic gentry families.[18] Mrs Barbara O'Connell, one of Nagle's most valuable lay assistants, was the daughter of a wealthy merchant and the wife of a Cork doctor. Widowed in 1788, Mrs O'Connell decided to devote her final years to piety and charitable works, sponsoring a second foundation of the Presentation Sisters in Cork and providing it with an endowment of 1,500 pounds.[19]

For Catholic as for Protestant women at this period philanthropy was primarily the preserve of the leisured, the affluent and the genteel. Most of those who engaged in such activity were women of independent means who chose to devote their time and fortune to good works. In doing so they drew on family, and specifically female, traditions of care for dependants and the local poor, as well as on the sense of responsibility felt by an emerging and increasingly affluent Catholic bourgeoisie for the disadvantaged of its own community, and for the wellbeing of the faith. There were, however, exceptions to this rule. Teresa Mulally, for instance, grew up in apparently prosperous circumstances, but as an adult had to support herself by working as a milliner. Lacking any personal fortune, she financed her projects from her savings and a lottery win of a few hundred pounds.[20] Bridget Burke, founder of the Townsend Street Asylum, was a 'working woman' of 'respectable . . . working-class' parentage. Widowed and with a young child to support, Burke earned her living for many years by working as a cook and later as a monthly nurse, and funded her shelter for 'fallen women' by setting up a 'penny collection' among friends and fellow servants. However, unlike Mulally, who retained a say in the running of her institution until her death, Burke seems to have had little control over the asylum she founded, and her name does not appear on a list of governesses of the charity published in 1821.[21]

Charitable works by lay members of the middle and lower orders of society were actively encouraged by the confraternities that were established in the course of the century in many urban areas. These associations had been a vital element in religious revival among the laity in Counter-Reformation Europe and had been introduced into Ireland in the early seventeenth century. The religious and civil conflicts of the time were a bar to their widespread establishment, but they were revived in the following century, becoming an indispensable agent of the Catholic resurgence among the laity. In Ireland, as elsewhere, women formed a major proportion of their membership, imbibed their doctrines of spiritual and social responsibility, and shared in their charitable endeavours. For example, the Confraternity of the Cord of St Francis, active in Wexford and Waterford in the second half of the century, had as its primary aim the revival of 'virtue and Christian piety', but members were also exhorted 'to help and do good to all that are in want', to comfort the poor, and to visit the sick and prisoners. Of 681 members listed for Wexford in the period 1763–89, 609 were female. Women were also admitted to membership of the Sodality of the Blessed Virgin Mary, and in the Dublin diocese in 1696 they outnumbered men by almost two to one. During the eighteenth century this society, which also prescribed works of mercy and charity, had branches in Waterford, Clonmel and Cork as well as Dublin. The Confraternity of Christian Doctrine, established in Wexford and in St Michan's parish in Dublin at the end of the century, was primarily concerned with the provision of religious instruction. Its membership in Dublin appears to have been largely female at this period, and all of the ninety-six teachers listed for St Michan's parish for the years 1799–1800 were women.[22]

The confraternities' educational projects reflect the Tridentine church's emphasis on religious education, which was, of course, traditionally an area of female responsibility. This was reinforced in the Irish context by the fact that the ban on Catholic education meant that for much of the century catechesis was largely home-based. Predictably, therefore, education, and particularly religious education, formed a major part of Catholic women's philanthropic activity. So Nagle, motivated by a conviction that 'I should run a very great risk of salvation if I did not follow the inspiration', and alarmed by what she perceived as the 'licentiousness' and 'ignorance of the lower classes', devised a regime for her schools that prioritised her pupils' spiritual development.[23] Having been taught to read, they learned the Catechism by heart and attended Mass daily. Nagle herself prepared them for First Communion, after which 'they go to Confession every month and to Communion when their confessors think proper'.[24] Anticipating the missionary initiatives of nineteenth-century Irish Catholicism by almost one hundred years, Nagle saw her educational project as having an evangelical potential that went far beyond the merely local. 'All my children', she wrote, 'are brought up to be fond of instructing, as I think it lies in the power of the poor to be of [more] service that way than the rich.' In sending boys from Cork to employment in the West Indies she urged them to 'take great pains with the little blacks to instruct them', and saw her schools, situated as they were in 'a place of such trade', as potentially 'of service to a great many parts of the world'. 'If I could be of any service in saving souls in any part of the globe', she declared, 'I would willingly do all in my power.'[25]

Mulally, too, regarded the religious education of her pupils as her primary responsibility:

From March until the latter end of September they came to school
at half past seven, joined in the morning prayer, went to 8 o'clock
Mass, returned and said the Hymn of the Holy Ghost. Next, they
answered their tasks of Catechism and spelling. Then they sat
down to work . . . until three o'clock. The Angelus and Acts at 12
o'clock, the Litany of the Blessed Virgin at three o'clock. They
broke up at three, and returned at four . . . No lessons were said in
the evening; sometimes one read a life of a saint . . . at other times,
explanations of words or the tables in Arithmetic. They concluded
at six o'clock with the psalm: 'Praise the Lord, ye children', and
some other short prayers.

Attendance was also required on Sundays and on holy days, 'for an hour
after the last Mass at an explanation of the catechism, by which means
many come to Mass on those days who otherwise would omit it'.[26]

However, both Nagle and Mulally were keenly aware of the need
to combine religious instruction with training that would equip those
in their care for their future roles in life. Indeed, Nagle specifically
expressed her desire that the pupils in the pay school that the
Ursulines were to set up should 'learn what was proper to teach
young ladies hereafter, as there is a general complaint both in this
kingdom and in England that the children are taught only to say their
prayers'. For the pupils in the poor schools, on the other hand, 'what
was proper to teach' was what would best fit them for employment.
Thus, the boys in Nagle's schools learned reading, writing and arithmetic, the girls reading and needlework.[27] Mulally, too, was keenly
aware of the need to supply her pupils with education and skills
'whereby they may be rendered useful to society, and capable of
earning honest bread for themselves', and, having supported herself
for many years by her own efforts, she must have had first-hand
experience of the dangers to which women were exposed by distress
and unemployment. Of the girls whom she wished to assist she wrote:
'their poverty, extreme as it is, is not the worst of their miseries. Their
chief misfortune is to be without any means of instruction, for want of
which they grow up in such habits of ignorance, idleness and vice, as
render them for ever after not only useless, but highly pernicious to
themselves and the public.'[28]

The sentiments expressed by Mulally in a letter written towards the
end of her life to Archbishop Troy encapsulate the complexity of

7. The room in Presentation Convent, George's Hill, where Teresa Mulally died in 1803. (Courtesy of the Presentation Sisters, George's Hill, Dublin).

motives behind virtually all eighteenth-century charity. Education provided to the poor, she wrote, should incorporate, 'besides . . . spiritual instruction', training in 'morality, decency and industry', qualities currently 'so much wanting among our poor'.[29] Mulally's philanthropy was inevitably coloured by her Catholicism in the context of late eighteenth-century Ireland, yet her concept of its ultimate purpose, as portrayed here, was one that was shared by the great majority of contemporary philanthropists, of whatever background or confession. Religion featured as a driving force among charitable women of all denominations, but so too did Enlightenment-derived humanitarian ideals, and an essentially conservative anxiety about the potential impact of poverty on society and religion. This apprehension was compounded for Catholic philanthropists by the much higher proportion of poor in the Catholic community and by the implications that this might have for the future development of the church.

In the focus of their charity and in the concerns motivating it, then, charitable Catholic women followed the general pattern of eighteenth-century female philanthropy. Their religion, however, subjected them to a number of difficulties not experienced by their Protestant counterparts, while the penal legislation, although it was rarely activated against Catholic projects, could never be entirely disregarded. As Nagle reminded Eleanor Fitzsimons, then serving her novitiate in Paris and preparing to become a member of the first Ursuline community in Ireland, 'we are in a country [in which] we can't do as we please'.[30] Nagle herself, while she flouted the law in setting up her schools, habitually acted with discretion, partly because unfavourable attention might interfere with her work, but also because she feared reprisals against members of her family. As leading members of the Catholic gentry with alleged Jacobite sympathies, the Nagles might well feel that their position was vulnerable, and Nano was particularly anxious about the possible implications for her uncle Joseph Nagle, 'who is, I think, the most disliked by the Protestants of any Catholic in the kingdom'.[31] While the Nagles seem to have suffered no ill effects as a result of Nano's initiatives, her fears serve as a reminder that, although official repression was largely a thing of the past by 1750, the institutional church and Irish Catholics generally were left with a sense of insecurity into the closing decades of the century. Indeed, the opening of her mission did coincide with a resurfacing of sectarian animosity in the Cork region, evidenced in tensions between Catholic and Protestant gentry, and in the harassment of individual Catholics.[32] Nano's enterprises attracted some anti-Catholic protests in the press and in 1772 the Cork Court of d'Oyer Hundred made an attempt to ban the introduction of the Ursulines to the city.[33] Despite the failure of this effort, Nagle continued to exercise caution in her dealings with the authorities and with the populace in general – in 1779, for instance, she opposed the Ursulines' decision to exchange the black gowns they had worn since their arrival for the religious habit.[34] In the following year the Presentation Sisters' transfer to a new house took place against the background of the anti-Catholic Gordon Riots in London, and Nagle took precautions to avoid the possibility of any similar demonstration at home:

When the disturbances broke out in London, I was afraid to venture, imagining the same contagious frenzy may break out in this kingdom. So [I] waited till the times seemed quite peaceful, yet notwithstanding we stole like thieves. I got up before three in the morning [and] had all our beds taken down and sent to the House, before any was up in the street. [I] begged of the ladies not to say a word about it to anyone . . . nor did [I] not let any person know it in the town of my friends, as I was sure [that by] acting in this manner the good work could be carried on much better than in making any noise about it.[35]

Mulally, too, defied the ban, which survived until 1782, on Catholics teaching school, but felt the impact of the penal legislation in relation to the financing of her operations. Restrictions on the endowment of Catholic institutions complicated, delayed and in some cases pre-vented the payment of legacies. A bequest intended by Mrs Coppinger for the support of the school at Mary's Lane had to be described in her will as being simply for the relief of the poor and, despite lengthy negotiations with the Bellew family, Mulally managed to secure payment of only the annual interest on the amount rather than the full sum of the bequest.[36] She herself, having sought legal advice on the validity of leaving her property in trust for her school, was informed that, although Catholics were now permitted to teach children of their own religion, 'yet there is a particular saving in that act, that nothing therein contained shall be construed to enable Roman Catholics to found any Popish endowed school'. In her will, drawn up in 1795, she left the major part of her estate to 'my two friends, Frances Doyle and Bridget Doran, spinsters' – in fact, Sister Mary Francis and Sister Ignatius of Nagle's Order of the Charitable Instruction, which had taken over the management of the school and orphanage in the previous year.[37]

The difficulties presented by the penal legislation, then, were irritat-ing but not insuperable, and both Nagle and Mulally encountered a more unexpected obstacle to their work in the hostility of elements within their own community. Mulally was accused of being 'an artful hypocrite, insinuating herself where there was any hope of getting money', and her offer of a site for a new church adjoining the convent at George's Hill created a bitter controversy within the parish and exposed her to 'misrepresentations' and 'calumny'.[38] This particular dispute was prolonged by the lengthy absence abroad of the parish priest and may have been intensified by rivalries that had developed

8. Presentation convent and school, George's Hill, Dublin. (Courtesy of the Presentation Sisters, George's Hill, Dublin).

in that vacuum, but the virulence of the dispute suggests considerable resentment on the part of some parishioners of Mulally's enterprise and assertiveness. Nagle, having decided to establish her schools, kept her intention 'a profound secret, as I knew, if it were spoken of, I should meet with opposition on every side, particularly from my immediate family, as in all appearance they would suffer from it'.[39] As already noted, these misgivings were unfounded and the Nagles, having learned of her enterprises, supported them generously. However, others were clearly less easily convinced. In his biography of Nagle (1794), Bishop Coppinger referred to 'selfish, narrow, envious machinations from a quarter where they could not be supposed to originate' and recorded the 'opprobrious insults' to which Nagle was subjected during her lifetime by unspecified opponents: 'she has been bitterly cursed in our streets as a mere impostor; she has been charged with having squandered her money upon the building of houses for the sole purpose of getting a name, and with deceiving the world by her throng of beggars' brats. Has it not even been said that her schools were a seminary of prostitution?'[40]

Given the continued need for discretion at a time when the penal legislation, however sporadically implemented, was still in force, it is probable that some Catholics, both lay and clerical, were wary of activities that might have the effect of focusing attention on their community. Moreover, while charitable women received useful support and encouragement from individual clerics, some members of the Catholic hierarchy were evidently reluctant to associate themselves with schemes that might be regarded as in any way subversive or even novel. Thus, Bishop Butler of Cork urged Nagle to obtain 'the Protestants' consent' for her establishment, advice that even the usually cautious Nagle rejected.[41] Twenty years later Bridget Burke sought guidance from spiritual advisers in establishing her asylum for penitent females, yet, 'until it was fairly launched, and there were well-founded hopes of its being permanently successful, it was thought not wise to place it publicly under the patronage of the Archbishop or any of the higher ecclesiastics'.[42]

However, while there were certainly practical reasons for discretion in the context of the times, the virulence of some of the criticism levelled at Nagle and Mulally suggests that at least some of their co-religionists regarded their activities – however apparently useful they might be to religion and society – as in some way unseemly or unacceptable. In eighteenth- and nineteenth-century Ireland, as in Counter-Reformation Europe, such assertiveness did not go unchallenged, and in the decades that followed ecclesiastical authorities made clear their determination that Catholic female charity should be permitted to flourish only within strictly defined limits. In practice this meant that the women involved must submit themselves, as professed religious, to clerical direction and control.

In her examination of nineteenth-century female philanthropy Maria Luddy has drawn attention to the process by which the expanding religious orders displaced Catholic laywomen from public charitable involvement. According to Luddy, 'after 1830 few Catholic lay women involved themselves publicly in the provision of charity. The charitable work of nuns became the public face of private philanthropic enterprise and the funds secured for them, particularly by lay women, allowed them to expand their range of enterprises while relegating these lay women to the subordinate role of fund-raisers.'[43]

In contrast, the Catholic contribution to eighteenth-century philanthropy was spearheaded, not by nuns, but by concerned and committed laywomen. This, however, may have been the result less of personal preference than of necessity, since none of the female religious orders operating in Ireland before the introduction of the Ursulines in 1771 had any formal involvement in practical social work. Although the penal legislation relating to Catholic education and the endowment of Catholic institutions was undoubtedly a disincentive to such activity, the Tridentine insistence on enclosure as an essential feature of the organisation of women's congregations was probably at least as significant. While convents, such as that of the Dominicans in Channel Row, were subject to periodic harassment during the first quarter of the century, they were later able to consolidate and even to modestly expand their position. The Dominicans, Carmelites and Augustinians ran boarding schools in Dublin for the daughters of the Catholic nobility and gentry, and enjoyed the patronage of ladies such as the Duchess of Tyrconnell and the Countess of Fingall.[44] Enclosure, however, offered a more serious obstacle to the involvement of nuns in charitable activity. Even in Catholic Europe the female religious orders were markedly unsuccessful in their efforts to establish an active apostolate, despite the fact that a number of them, including the Ursulines and Mary Ward's Institute of the Blessed Virgin Mary, had been founded specifically for that purpose.[45] As young women

9. Portrait of Teresa Mulally with children, date unknown, Presentation Convent, George's Hill, Dublin. (Courtesy of the Presentation Sisters, George's Hill, Dublin).

both Nagle and Mulally claimed a vocation to the religious life, but both drew back from entering any of the existing orders, almost certainly because of the limitations that membership would have placed on their philanthropic calling. Both women, however, from an early stage in their careers, expressed a desire to place their respective projects in the hands of a religious congregation that would be capable of maintaining them. The difficulty lay in finding one whose rule permitted it to do so. Ultimately Nagle was led to a realisation of the need for a new type of sisterhood that would be free to engage in active charitable and social work.

From about 1767 Nagle and her chief clerical ally, Dr Francis Moylan, were engaged in negotiations with the Ursulines in Paris with a view to establishing a house of the order in Cork. The first Ursulines arrived in the city in 1771 and in the following year they opened a boarding school for the daughters of wealthy Catholics. However, the sisters were prevented by their rule of enclosure from taking over supervision of the poor schools and other projects that Nagle had intended to place in their care. Determined to safeguard the future of her charities, in 1775 Nagle created a new congregation, the Society of the Charitable Instruction. As members of a sisterhood bound by simple vows and with freedom to leave the convent, its members were 'to be devoted solely to works of charity among the poor; and . . . to seek them out in their hovels of misery and want and woe' – in short, to carry on Nagle's mission as she had originally envisaged it.[46]

The foundation of the Society marked the opening of a remarkable period of expansion in Irish female religious life, and served as a model for the missionary and social role of nuns in nineteenth-century Ireland. While the older enclosed orders expanded their sphere of activity to include teaching, nursing and welfare work, the new native congregations, such as the Sisters of Charity (1813) and the Sisters of Mercy (1831), had from their foundation a clearly social purpose, and their founders, Mary Aikenhead and Catherine McAuley, were themselves initially prompted to activity by precisely that impulse of pious benevolence that had characterised the initiatives of Nagle, Mulally, Burke and their associates.[47]

For the women involved there were clear advantages in deciding to integrate themselves more fully into the structures of the church. Both Nagle and Mulally, in embarking on their projects, sought the assistance of similarly minded women and established what were in effect lay sisterhoods, united by religious zeal and by a philanthropic impulse. To formalise this arrangement by the establishment of a religious community would be to create an enduring and stable framework within which the initiatives taken might be maintained. As Mother Angela Collins remarked to Teresa Mulally, in discussing the handover of the latter's school to a new foundation of the Presentation Sisters, 'it's after your death there may be danger of the permanency of this great work'.[48] Nagle, too, saw the establishment of a religious congregation as the most effective and desirable means of safeguarding her work, and took the view that instruction in the faith should be in the hands of religious rather than lay people. Following the establishment of her congregation she dismissed almost all the lay schoolmistresses whom she had previously employed.[49] According to Moylan:

> She prudently foresaw . . . that a work of this extensive charity could not long subsist, unless the persons charged with the Instruction considered it as a duty, and attended to it, not for a salary, but from motives of religion and zeal for God's glory – after recommending the matter to God by long and fervent prayer she judged the establishment of a Religious Community necessary to perpetuate the good work.[50]

Despite initial financial difficulties and a shortage of recruits, the Sisters of the Charitable Instruction established a convent at George's Hill in 1794, taking over the management of Mulally's school there, and by 1800 they had houses at Killarney, Waterford and Kilkenny, as well as a second convent in Cork. As the Presentation Order they went on to operate convents and schools throughout Ireland and England, as well as in North America, Australia, New Zealand, Africa and the Indian subcontinent. Alongside this apparent success, however, the history of the order offers a clear example of the limitations that membership of a religious congregation could place on the effectiveness of its members. As a laywoman Nagle had been free to disregard Moylan's objections to her plan to found her own community – according to the Presentation Annals, she ignored his threats and 'spiritedly pursued the work of God in defiance of his efforts to prevent it'.[51] A religious congregation, on the other hand, was subject both to its own rule and to episcopal authority, either of which could conflict with philanthropic practice. Thus, Teresa Mulally, like Nagle before her, was dismayed by the restrictions that this imposed on her mission. Just a few months after the sisters took over the running of her school she complained that the spiritual exercises required of them interfered with their teaching commitments. As the Annals of the House put it:

> She was so ardently zealous for the instruction of the poor that . . . the nuns . . . found it difficult to make her understand that the principal and general end of all religious orders should be first the perfecting of themselves in the way of the Lord.[52]

However, the imposition of enclosure on the congregation in 1805 introduced a more serious limitation on its members' scope for action. The decision of the sisters to seek a change in status from a congregation with simple vows to a religious order with solemn vows and enclosure was taken on the advice of 'some learned and pious ecclesiastics',[53] and was probably motivated by a desire to regularise their position and to encourage recruitment. Its effect, however, was to remove them from all charitable involvement other than the provision of education for poor girls within their enclosure, a restriction that ran directly counter to Nagle's founding intentions.

Nagle's foundation marked the high point and heralded the close of this 'matriarchal era' within Irish Catholicism. As religious, charitable Catholic women found their independence and ability to innovate curtailed by canonical and episcopal authority. 'In this way', as Caitriona Clear points out, 'these organisations were brought under the control of the Church, their leaders subjected to the Church's discipline and their, in many cases considerable, resources of expertise and confidence harnessed to a church which was increasing in political and economic power'.[54]

The piety that was a major element in their motivation must have inclined charitable women to accept the limitations on their autonomy involved in membership of a religious congregation. So, too, must the tangible benefits of integration, which included the promise of permanence, and the encouragement of donations and recruits. For the individuals themselves there could also be a gain. As Olwen Hufton has pointed out, the 'scope for professionalisation' that religious life offered to Catholic women provided status, occupation and an alternative to marriage that was envied by many of their

10. Crypt of Presentation Convent, George's Hill, Dublin. Teresa Mulally was buried here, as were Presentation Sisters until 1913. The plaque commemorates Teresa Mulally as well as Fr Mulcaile (d. 1801), Mulally's co-workers, Anne Corballis (d. 1793) and Catherine Toole (d. 1806), and benefactor Mrs Clare Knowd (d. 1813). (Courtesy of the Presentation Sisters, George's Hill, Dublin).

Protestant sisters.[55] Nuns' contributions in the fields of education, health care and poor relief in nineteenth-century Ireland offered persuasive proof of their usefulness, and provided vindication of the decision to operate as religious rather than as laywomen – but that contribution, while it won them acclaim from hierarchy, clergy and laity, failed to win them admission to the power structures of a patriarchal and increasingly authoritarian church. Moreover, the close identification that developed at this stage between the religious and the philanthropic missions resulted in a narrowing of the range of choices available to Catholic laywomen, as membership of a religious

order became in effect a pre-condition for involvement in social and charitable work, imposed by a church that valued, but sought to maintain strict control over, its female members' contributions.

The recovery of Irish Catholicism from the disruptions of the penal era coincided with a significant expansion in charitable activity by

1766 An Address to the Charitable
Of St Michan's Parish.

GHAD/FD/46

Among the real Objects of this Parish there are none whose necessities require more to be considered, than the poor Children of the Female Sex.

They are, many of them, Orphans, and the rest, by the helpless condition of their Parents, scarce better than Orphans. They suffer all the hardships of extreme Poverty: but their Poverty, extreme as it is, is not the worst of their miseries. Their chief misfortune is to be without any means of Instruction; for want of which they grow up in such habits of Ignorance, Idleness and Vice, as render them for ever after not only useless, but highly pernicious to themselves and the Publick.

It was thought they might receive some benefit by assisting, as they did for some time, at the Charity-School established for the poor Boys. But, besides the danger of uniting both Sexes in one School, it was found by experience that a Man is ill qualified for such a task as the tuition of Girls, which requires the peculiar abilities of a discreet and skilfull Woman.

Such a Woman is now employed, and has been so since last May in a convenient place, which was then hired and fitted out for a School. She has under her care a certain number of the aforesaid poor Girls, whom she instructs in their Prayers and Catechism, in reading and writing, knitting, quilting, mantua-making, plain-work &c whereby they may be rendered usefull to Society, and capable of earning honest bread for themselves.

Such a School, so long wanting, and so happily commenced has nothing to support it, but what it expects from the Charity of the Faithfull. Though it hopes encouragement from all good Parishioners, its chief dependance is on the Ladies, whose usual tenderness for the Poor in General, can not but show a particular feeling for the distressed members

11. First page of 'An address to the charitable of St Michan's Parish', issued by Teresa Mulally in 1766, beginning, 'Among the real Objects of this Parish, there are none whose necessities require more to be considered, than the poor Children of the Female Sex . . .'. (Courtesy of the Presentation Sisters, George's Hill, Dublin).

women of all religious denominations. Common features of this philanthropy included its concentration on the condition of poor women and children, and the blend of religious zeal and social concern that inspired it. Within this context a number of Catholic women created structures of relief that benefited the needy and marginalised of their own community, and promoted Catholic teaching, practice and values throughout society. It should be noted, moreover, that these efforts were undertaken in the face of dual disadvantage. While their faith left them exposed to the provisions of the anti-Catholic legislation, which had the power to impede if not to prevent their initiatives, their assertiveness made them suspect in the eyes of those within their own church who took the view that female activism must be subject to canonical control. Ultimately, like their co-religionists elsewhere in Counter-Reformation Europe, charitable Catholic women accepted the restrictions inherent in membership of a religious congregation as the price to be paid for the survival of their projects and for continued permission to be active, and in doing so they set the pattern for the Catholic female philanthropy of the next century. With hindsight the surrender of autonomy that this entailed may be regretted. For the women concerned, however, it was surely a necessary compromise, given the impulse that motivated their 'pious occupations', their determination to perpetuate them, and their commitment to the expansion of their efforts on behalf of the faith to 'other parts of the Kingdom' and beyond.

DISCOVERING IRISH NUNS IN THE NINETEENTH-CENTURY UNITED STATES: THE CASE OF CHICAGO

Suellen Hoy

Despite my Irish roots and Catholic schooling, it was not until 1991–92, while living in Dublin, that I discovered (professionally speaking) Irish nuns in the United States. That may not surprise you, if you are familiar with US history textbooks or collections of readings and documents used in women's history courses from coast to coast. Although minorities and women of nearly every kind have been included, Catholic sisters are curiously absent. Yet they may have been the most publicly active women of the nineteenth and early twentieth centuries. After taking stock of their charitable, educational, health and social service institutions, Leslie Woodcock Tentler rebuked historians of women in 1993 for their lack of interest in nuns: 'Had women under secular or Protestant auspices compiled this record of achievement', she remarked, 'they would be today a thoroughly researched population.'[1]

When I arrived in Dublin with my historian husband in August 1991 I had never seriously considered the accomplishments of Catholic sisters either in Ireland or in the United States. Instead, I was more interested in religion as a motive for emigration. Specifically, I wanted to know about religious communities and their 'major drives . . . to gain new members', as described by Hasia Diner in her study of Irish immigrant women in the nineteenth-century United States.[2] After a year of research and writing in Ireland I had learned a great deal about the emigration and recruitment of women as missionaries to the United States, and I presented those findings in 'The journey Out', an essay in the *Journal of Women's History*.[3] Once I was home again, on the outskirts of Chicago, new questions demanded answers: what happened to the thousands of good and adventuresome young women after they left Ireland? How did they adjust away from home?

50

How well did they do, living and working in US cities? I decided to take a look at Chicago, where early on, as Ellen Skerrett has noted, 'Irish Catholics claimed a distinct place for themselves . . . and left their imprint on the urban landscape.'[4]

EVERYWHERE, ACTIVE AND INDEFATIGABLE

Chicago's Irish Sisters of Mercy, when remembered in 1908 for their nursing during the city's cholera epidemics, were described as 'everywhere, active and indefatigable, visiting and ministering with tender solicitude to the afflicted sufferers'.[5] In 1992, as I began my search for Irish nuns, I also found them everywhere and active. By the end of the nineteenth century communities of Irish women religious, who came to Chicago early, were many and involved in a wide variety of enterprises, especially during times when Protestant women remained close to home and refused to walk the streets of poor neighbourhoods unescorted by a man. I also discovered that, through their indefatigability and commitment, these Irish nuns created a web of services that over time gave them a large and visible presence in a city shaped by sacred space. According to Skerrett, 'the Irish left their mark [on Chicago] not in words but in stone – Catholic churches, schools, convents, rectories, charitable institutions, and hospitals'.[6] The Sisters of Mercy provide the most obvious example of how Irish nuns contributed to this phenomenon.

On 23 September 1846 five Sisters of Mercy arrived in Chicago and established themselves as the first and, for the next ten years, the only community of nuns in the city. Sister Agatha (Margaret) O'Brien, born in County Carlow in 1822, was appointed Superior. She and the other four travelled to Chicago in the company of the Bishop of Chicago's brother and Mother Frances Warde, the American founder who had led the Mercys to Pittsburgh from Ireland in 1843. After several days Mother Frances returned to Pittsburgh and left the future of this frontier foundation in the hands of Sister Agatha, then only twenty-four years old.

Like many educated young women who would join the Mercys in cities across the United States, Sister Agatha came from a poor family. One of seventeen children of a cooper, she began religious life as a lay sister (a nun without dowry) and worked in the convent kitchen until volunteering in 1844 to join the first group of Sisters of Mercy to emigrate to the United States. The Irish-born Bishop Michael O'Connor, who invited them to Pittsburgh and crossed the Atlantic with them, recognised Sister Agatha's potential. Not wanting her talent restricted to domestic duties 'because her father happened to be a poor man in Ireland', he recommended that she be professed as a choir nun. As such, he later remarked, she was 'capable of ruling a nation'.[7]

When the Sisters of Mercy arrived in Chicago it was a primitive western outpost of fewer than 20,000 people. Here this small community of women religious became the church's shock troops (the St Vincent de Paul Society did not begin until 1857) to the thousands of desperate emigrants who escaped Ireland's Great Famine. Settled in a convent at Wabash and Madison near the city's centre, the nuns had 'not a moment to spare', according to Sister Agatha, because of the pressing needs of the many destitute Irish labourers who regularly arrived in Chicago during the late 1840s and 1850s.[8] These uninvited and frequently despised newcomers secured public works jobs on railroads and canals, and lived nearby in makeshift shanties. Dirty, uneducated and Catholic, they found themselves branded as alien, and 'a threat to American values, culture, and institutions'.[9] The Protestant majority did its best to keep at a safe distance from them, especially when the public's health was threatened.

During the summer of 1849 a cholera epidemic struck and spread along the Illinois and Michigan Canal. The Mercys were by then operating three schools, teaching Sunday school in several parishes, holding classes for illiterate adults, volunteering at a free dispensary opened by Rush Medical College and running an informal employment bureau for Irish women. However, knowing that the poor and the sick 'need help today, not next week', they set aside many of their routine activities and began nursing cholera victims. Their dedicated care of strangers as well as friends enhanced their public image and ensured their visibility. They went 'everywhere', always walking, and became known to Chicagoans, as they had to Dubliners, as the 'walking nuns'.[10]

When the outbreak ended and the sisters' nursing care was less in demand they agreed to take charge of Chicago's first Catholic orphanage, 'a haven for children who had lost their parents to the epidemic'. Two years later Sister Agatha accepted control of what

12. Sister Agatha [Margaret] O'Brien (1822–54) was first superior of the Sisters of Mercy in Chicago. Born into a poor family in Carlow, she laid the foundation for today's Mercy Hospital and St Xavier University. She died in one of Chicago's worst cholera epidemics. (Courtesy of the Sisters of Mercy, Chicago).

would become a landmark institution, Mercy Hospital, and a second orphanage.[11] Forty-four strong by then, and largely Irish, the Sisters of Mercy continued to staff two free schools, an academy (which later became St Xavier University) and three Sunday schools. Not surprisingly, during 1850–51 Sister Agatha wrote repeatedly that 'time is real precious here', that 'my hands are full', that 'we are very busy' and 'greatly pressed for time'. Perhaps more astonishing was that the sisters had 'so much to do with Protestants'. At St Xavier Academy, where 'almost all the children' were Protestant, the Sisters of Mercy made 'some very warm friends among them'.[12]

In the eight years before her death at the age of thirty-two in the cholera epidemic of 1854 Sister Agatha and her colleagues created at Wabash and Madison something of a social settlement – the sort that most Americans have come to identify with Chicago in the late nineteenth century. Yet this competent and committed woman religious completed her life's work before either Jane Addams or Ellen Gates Starr, the founders of Hull House, were born. By 1889, when Hull House opened on Halsted Street, hundreds of Catholic nuns – not all Mercys, but the majority from Irish working-class families – had already shown Chicagoans how single women could live useful lives among the poor. Yet for historians of American women, or even Chicagoans, when Catholic sisters are mentioned or the name of Agatha O'Brien is recalled almost nothing of historical significance comes to mind.[13]

WORK FOR WOMAN'S GOOD

Another less obvious but equally notable community of Irish nuns in nineteenth-century Chicago were the Sisters of the Good Shepherd. In September 1889, one week after Jane Addams and Ellen Gates Starr began Hull House, the Good Shepherd Sisters established the Chicago Industrial School for Girls. This was their second charitable institution in the city. Thirty years earlier, in May 1859, four Irish-born sisters had opened the House of the Good Shepherd – its name when incorporated in 1867 – as a 'magdalen asylum', whose purpose was to reform 'abandoned women'. Over the years the nuns extended their care from women accused of prostitution or disorderly conduct to delinquent and dependent girls.[14]

13. The Mercy Convent at Carlow, from which Sister Agatha O'Brien and six others emigrated to the United States in 1844. Invited to Pittsburgh by the Cork-born bishop, Michael O'Connor, this group became the first community of Sisters of Mercy in the United States. (Courtesy of the Sisters of Mercy, Chicago).

The Sisters of Our Lady of Charity of the Good Shepherd were a semi-cloistered order with origins in seventeenth-century France. After establishing a central headquarters in Angers in 1835 they spread throughout France and to many cities across the world. 'Your zeal', said St Euphrasia Pelletier, founder and first superior general, 'must not be contented with one town, one foundation; it must comprise all lands and all peoples.'[15] By the end of the nineteenth century Good Shepherd Sisters were found in nearly 200 convents, most of them in the United States, Ireland and Great Britain.

Despite their French beginnings, Chicago's Good Shepherd Sisters were made up almost entirely of Irish and Irish-American women. With few exceptions – notably a remarkable French-Canadian woman, Mother Mary Nativity Noreau, whose term as superior of the House of the Good Shepherd lasted fifteen years (1864–79) – a large majority of the professed sisters had Irish parents. As noted above, the first four who came to Chicago in 1859 were Irish-born; fifty-one years later, in 1910, thirty-three of the forty-one nuns at the House of the Good Shepherd had Irish parents and ten had been born in Ireland. An additional four had one Irish parent; only one sister had parents both of whom were born in the United States. Across town at the Chicago Industrial School fifteen of nineteen Good Shepherd Sisters had Irish parents; five of them had been born in Ireland. Not a single one had parents who were both born in the United States.[16]

During the nineteenth century, first at the House of the Good Shepherd and then at their Industrial School for Girls, Chicago's Good Shepherds provided shelter, religious instruction, vocational training and job placement for thousands of women and girls who either had no home or were sent to them by relatives or the courts. Some had been prostitutes; others were convicted of intoxication, disorderly conduct or vagrancy; and most of them had probably shown signs of 'immorality' or lack of control by using obscene language, coming home late at night or associating with individuals of questionable character. All were poor – a large majority were daughters of immigrants (Irish and German first; then Polish, French, and Italian by the turn of the century) along with a few African Americans and mulattos – and unable to find work that paid well.[17]

Despite the unmistakeable presence of Catholic sisters and their charges, it is generally believed that Irish bishops and priests built the Catholic Church in America during the nineteenth century. In Chicago, for example, Irish bishops dominated into the early twentieth century: 'from the appointment of the first bishop, William Quarter, in 1844 until the death of Archbishop James Quigley in 1915, all the bishops of Chicago were either Irish-born or of Irish parentage, with the exception of Bishop James Van De Velde, a Belgian who briefly presided over the diocese from 1849 to 1859.' Parish priests of Irish heritage were less dominant in Chicago, but in 1902 they headed sixty-three parishes out of a total of 132. However, once hundreds of nuns are stirred into this urban mix it becomes increasingly clear that the growth of American Catholicism depended heavily on their committed service.[18]

It is impossible to state the exact number of Irish women who emigrated to the United States during the nineteenth century as sisters or with the intention of entering a religious community. It seems safe to say that, at a minimum, 4,000 or 5,000 did so; and perhaps as many as 7,000. What is known for certain is that they normally came

14. In 1907, the Sisters of the Good Shepherd moved to this newly-constructed House of the Good Shepherd on Chicago's North Side. Since 1859, the Good Shepherds had cared first for abandoned women and later for dependent and delinquent girls. Today, at the same address, they provide shelter for battered women and their children. (Courtesy of the Sisters of the Good Shepherd, Chicago).

in groups and at the invitation of a bishop, priest or nun, almost all of whom were also Irish. But not all Irish nuns were recruited as adults in Ireland. Many came to the United States as children and subsequently joined religious congregations; others entered orders in France or elsewhere in Europe and later found themselves assigned to American missions. Still others, daughters of Irish immigrants, were born in the United States and attended parochial schools, often staffed by Irish-born nuns. At some point these women decided to become members of the communities they knew best – those of their teachers, sodality sponsors or relatives. Although their journeys to the United States and to the religious life may have been different, they shared a heritage that was both Irish and Catholic.[19]

Over time the majority of Irish and Irish-American nuns also tended to come from working-class families. Immigrants themselves or the daughters of immigrants, they were attracted to the religious life in the United States because it offered them a full range of opportunities. In Ireland, without dowries, they could become only lay sisters, but in the United States, where the need for women religious was so great, the dowry ceased to be a requirement. By the late nineteenth century 'education' had replaced 'dowry' as the all-important word.[20] Thus, in Chicago and other cities the socioeconomic disparity between Irish nuns and their clientele was usually much less than that between Protestant reformers (who were almost always middle-class) and theirs. Might this difference have accounted for a deeper understanding on the sisters' part? Let us take a look at a controversy that occurred in Chicago in the 1890s between the Sisters of the Good Shepherd and the Illinois Woman's Alliance.

The Alliance, organized in 1888, achieved a number of reforms before it was dissolved six years later, yet historians of American women know more about it than about the House of the Good Shepherd, now 140 years old. Nevertheless, because of its intentions, the Alliance quickly succeeded in bringing together delegates from nearly every woman's organisation in Chicago. Its main purpose was to assist working women and their children by building more schools and public baths, enforcing compulsory education laws and factory inspection ordinances, and ending child labour. It also called for fairer treatment of prostitutes and argued that women should not be convicted of prostitution 'unless the men involved were willing to come forward and bear witness against them'.[21]

From what evidence exists it appears that the Illinois Woman's Alliance did not disapprove of the work of the House of the Good Shepherd or its Protestant counterpart, the Erring Woman's Refuge (1863).[22] Yet in December 1890 one member of the Alliance registered a severe criticism against the House of the Good Shepherd. She charged publicly that the sisters held some inmates against their will and 'deprived [them] of their liberty' in order to receive 'the ten-dollar monthly allowance for their board' from the county. The nuns were 'much annoyed' by the accusation. Thomas Brenan, a lawyer and long-time friend, spoke initially on their behalf, explaining that residents at the House of the Good Shepherd were 'at liberty to leave whenever they chose'. Then Mother Holy Cross McCabe told the press that, although she had at times persuaded women in their care to remain longer, they were free to leave when they had served their sentences.[23]

Although both the Sisters of the Good Shepherd and the Illinois Woman's Alliance had the interests of poor women at heart, their views of what was best for them were diametrically opposed. There seems little doubt that in this instance middle-class and working-class cultures had clashed. Representatives of the Alliance contended that 'the right to personal liberty' was the issue, but the sisters disagreed. They believed that many of their residents – especially older women who were uneducated, unskilled and lacked family support – would simply not be 'free' in the streets of Chicago. From the Good Shepherds' perspective the city offered poor women more opportunities for degradation and failure than it did for freedom and success. Knowing how tenacious the tag of 'immorality' could be for women, the sisters had deliberately and carefully protected the privacy of those who came to them. Yet, despite their commitment and care, the Good Shepherd Sisters knew also that their programme of reclamation did not always provide an easy route to a free and full life in American society. After this public disagreement they must also have realised that religion, ethnicity and class could make for wide divergences of opinion.

The sisters were fortunate that the attack by the Illinois Woman's Alliance received comparatively few headlines. Perhaps it was dismissed because, by the 1890s, the Good Shepherds' 'measure of success' was well-known and appreciated by Protestants and Catholics alike. In 1891 they cared for nearly 500 troubled women and girls in quarters that were crowded. Thus, during the following year Mother Holy Cross McCabe borrowed 15,000 dollars and purchased ten acres of wooded property at Grace and Racine Streets, the present location of the House of the Good Shepherd, where battered women and their children now find shelter. In December 1896, two years after the demise of the Illinois Woman's Alliance, the sisters opened the House of the Good Shepherd to the public for the first time in its history. More than 2,000 Chicagoans visited this unique institution and contributed generously to the nuns' 'Donation Party', following notice from the *Chicago Tribune* that 'their work is for woman's good'.[24]

AN APPEALING ALTERNATIVE

Jane Addams was among the influential Protestant and Catholic women who toured the House of the Good Shepherd during its December open house. No doubt she honoured the achievements of the Irish nuns who had built, while she and Ellen Gates Starr were still only girls, a recognised charitable institution for the most despised of Chicago's immigrant poor.[25] The Good Shepherds, like the Mercys, had used their religious convictions, and their concern for women and children, not only to create respectable roles for themselves, but

15. A study-hall of dependent girls at the House of the Good Shepherd (*c.*1908), where they learned 'the three Rs' and took classes in religion and music. (Courtesy of the Sisters of the Good Shepherd, Chicago).

also to enlarge the public dimension of their work. In the process they offered Catholic women an appealing alternative to the life choices available to most American women at the time.

Earlier in the century Protestant reformers such as Catharine Beecher and Mary Livermore had looked with admiration and envy at the lives of pioneering nuns on the western frontier. In a place and at a time when opportunities to save souls and do good were limitless, Catholic sisters had 'freedoms unknown to most other nineteenth-century women'.[26] The pace and competence with which these nuns built needed and respected urban institutions – generally free of male management – sparked the yearnings of numerous unmarried women who wanted to do something important in life. Some may have seen the religious life as an adventure or even as an escape, but most entered convents because they felt called by God to a life of service in the church and because they wanted to expand 'the narrow range of what was possible for women who were coming of age' more than a hundred years ago.[27] First- and second-generation Irish women, whose hearts 'went out to the world in charitable intent', chose what families and friends often considered 'the better part'; they also enlarged their sphere and filled it with challenges.[28]

However, unlike well-spoken Protestant women reformers of the late nineteenth century, who in large numbers became involved in the temperance, settlement house and women's movements, the Mercys and Good Shepherds claimed no public voice. They were, after all, products of their religious training and members of a patriarchal Irish church. Following the US bishops' decision in 1884 that every parish should open a school Catholic sisters readily responded to what was defined as the church's critical need. Thus, over time their ministries became less varied and most women religious became teachers in parochial schools.

Throughout the nineteenth century, like other Irish-American women, Irish nuns had 'behaved aggressively and valued their economic prowess'. Yet, despite the support network they created for so many women of such varied circumstances, they frequently 'turned a cold shoulder to the organised women's rights movement'.[29] The leaders of this movement were, of course, middle-class Protestant women of Anglo-Saxon stock. This may help explain why the Irish nuns who laid such a solid foundation for nineteenth-century social reform have had almost no place in the historiography of American women.

In *New Catholic Women* Mary Jo Weaver contends that in the United States all Catholic women (lay as well as religious) have remained historically invisible because of 'the tendency of historians to ignore religion in general and Catholicism in particular'.[30] However, the sisters themselves must also bear a share of the blame for their omission. In short, they never claimed their rightful place in history. Often they were simply too busy, too overwhelmed with work, to think of their legacy; they also learned not to look to contemporaries for recognition. Thus, with limited time and energy, and a spirituality that emphasised humility and detachment, they kept their eyes on the one prize that truly mattered to them: their salvation and that of those they served. Nevertheless, those of us who are aware of the spirited lives and rich legacy of Irish nuns in the nineteenth-century United States must see that they are not forgotten.

GENDER, PUBLIC DISORDER AND THE SALVATION ARMY IN IRELAND, 1880–82

Janice Holmes

The Salvation Army was unique among nineteenth-century denominations in the formal and public roles that it assigned to women. Because of the attitudes of the founders, William and Catherine Booth, women were able to take on leadership positions and played a crucial role in the Army's strategy for denominational expansion. Between 1878 and 1890 the Army grew at a dramatic pace, from a small mission in the East End of London to an international movement with branches in more than twenty countries. Women were at the forefront of this massive endeavour.

Ireland was one of the first countries that the Army moved into during this period. In May 1880 four English women under the command of Caroline Reynolds landed in Belfast and began immediately to 'preach the gospel' among their target audience, the poor and the unchurched. By the time Reynolds moved on, in September 1882, she and thirty-four other women had established fifteen 'corps' (the Army's term for a congregation) across the North of Ireland.

The fact that the Salvation Army was using women to conduct public meetings and lead processions through the streets was highly unusual, and provoked a great deal of local comment about the propriety of women occupying such public roles. It was the public order implications of their presence that caused these Army women, and the communities in which they operated, the greatest difficulty. As the Army women began to move beyond the working-class streets of Belfast to towns such as Londonderry and Enniskillen, they frequently encountered violent mobs, composed largely of the 'lower orders', determined to disrupt their processions and their religious services.

Much of this behaviour was highly ritualised and resembled the traditional customs of 'charivari' or 'rough musicing'. However, in both Londonderry and Enniskillen this popular antagonism began to take on distinctly local forms. In Londonderry the Army quickly became the issue around which Catholic mobs and self-appointed Protestant bodyguards regularly clashed. In Enniskillen the actions of the Salvation Army provoked a serious row between local magistrates, who were members of the Church of Ireland, and a number of leading businessmen, who were Methodists and more sympathetic to the Army's methods than the magistrates were.

As members of what seemed to many Victorians a highly unorthodox organisation, the women who arrived in Ireland were prepared for violence. However, they were not prepared for the particularly 'Irish' dimension to that violence. In both Londonderry and Enniskillen the Army (unwittingly, I suggest) found itself caught between two rival sets of opinions. Members discovered that their public activity could have quite different outcomes in a society deeply divided along religious lines. As one Irish paper noted, 'We do not doubt in large English towns, where the mass of working classes neglect places of worship and profess the same creed, the outdoor service of song is found useful and attractive . . . But Enniskillen is very different, and street singing is here apt to cause religious rancour and foster bigotry.'[1]

On more than one occasion, in fact, the Salvation Army expressed its pride in its members' lack of cultural awareness. Given the violent consequences of their Irish work, one female officer remarked, 'Just as well, perhaps, that simple women, utterly ignorant of all the countless political and religious complications of the country, pioneered it!'[2] These were, however, more than just 'simple women'. Uneducated they may have been, and untrained in the skills of pulpit oratory, but between them they laid the foundation upon which an entire denomination was built. Unfortunately the religious divisions within nineteenth-century Irish society overshadowed the magnitude of their achievement. The fact that it was women in charge of this religious effort – unusual behaviour by any standard – was virtually ignored in favour of the public order implications of their activity.

BACKGROUND

The origins of the Salvation Army date back to 1865, when William Booth, a former minister in the Methodist New Connection, was invited to conduct a series of open-air meetings in the East End of London. Booth and his wife Catherine were both active evangelists who had been leading professional revival missions since 1861. Soon Booth's London meetings had become a permanent missionary effort among the working classes, which by 1870 was known as the Christian Mission. The original structure of the Mission was based on the Methodist model, with stations, circuits and annual conferences that all Mission workers attended. In 1878, however, this structure was overhauled and Booth was declared 'commander-in-chief' or, more commonly, the 'General'. The Mission was now called the Salvation Army and was organised along military lines. The basic unit was the 'corps', each with its own 'citadel', which was run by full-time, paid 'officers'. Regular members were known as 'soldiers'.

In theological terms the Salvation Army was firmly evangelical. It wanted to save souls and in order to achieve this it aimed 'only to preach the repentance of sins'.[3] It relied heavily on methods in common use in the nineteenth century, such as open-air services, public processions and gospel services in secular buildings. In several important respects, however, its practices set it apart from other denominations. First of all, the Army's use of military metaphors and its adoption of a military hierarchy was unique within Victorian Christianity. Secondly, the Army's focus on reaching out to the working classes and its willingness to employ working-class people in its efforts were also distinctive. Thirdly, and most importantly, the Army allowed women to occupy formal leadership roles within its ranks. It was the only denomination in the nineteenth century that officially endorsed and fostered the use of female leaders.

This was in large part due to the influence of Catherine Booth. Born Catherine Mumford in Ashbourne, Derbyshire, in 1829, by the age of twenty-six she had come to the conclusion that women, as human beings, were equal to men. In 1859 she published her ideas in a pamphlet in which she defended the public preaching of Phoebe Palmer, an American evangelist, as her right 'as part of the contract between God and humanity'.[4] This position was highly unusual. Although female preaching had been a notable feature of early Methodism, the justification for this behaviour had always rested on the notion of an 'extraordinary call' from God to such a public role. For Catherine, however, female preaching did not need to rely on exceptions: according to her, 'women could possess spiritual authority as women and could preach as Christian women in their own voices as a part of the natural order'.[5] After she and William moved to London she began to preach in public, and when they formed the Christian Mission it institutionalised leadership roles for women from the start. By late 1877 women were leading nine out of a total of thirty-six stations.[6] By 1878 roughly half of all Army officers were women and forty-six of them were leading their own corps.[7]

The reorganisation of the Christian Mission into the Salvation Army in 1878 put William Booth in sole charge of Army policy. This greatly facilitated the rapid expansion of the Army from a London-based to an international organisation. In 1868 there were nine Christian Mission stations. By 1870 eight more had been established and by the end of 1878 the total had grown to eighty-one. By 1886 there were more than 1,006 corps in the United Kingdom, and almost as many in Ireland, the United States, France and Scandinavia.[8]

It is not entirely clear why Booth decided to begin what he called a 'definite and organised effort in Dear Old Ireland'.[9] In his letter of invitation to the commissioning service for the Irish work he wrote:

> For a long time our attention has been directed to Ireland as offering a particularly needy field for the operation of the Army. Earnest Christians, both there and in various parts of England, have written urging us to send workers who should, in all simplicity, seek to reach the lower classes in the Irish cities, who have been represented to us as needing the simple preaching of the Gospel as much as any people in the world.[10]

Although the move to Ireland was delayed by the opening of work in the United States, by May 1880 the preparations had been completed, the halls secured and the officers selected. Booth appointed Major Caroline Reynolds as the leader of the Army's Irish effort. She was 'one of my most tried and experienced Officers', and had been a member of the Army from its earliest days. On 3 May 1880 she and four other female officers – Captains Phoebe Strong, Elizabeth Spencer, Mary Ann Marshall and Polly Flinn – were commissioned to the work in Ireland at a special meeting at Army headquarters. The next day they set sail and they landed in Belfast on 7 May 1880.

The Army's objectives in Ireland were straightforward, if somewhat naïve. Reynolds was told to 'point her guns against sin, and by the power of Jesu's name, to turn men from darkness to light, and from the power of Satan unto God'. In this task, Booth stressed, her methods were to be completely non-sectarian: she was 'not going to war against priestcraft, or Romanism, or Protestantism, or any other ism, unless it be sinfulism – but against SIN'.[11] Nevertheless, her ultimate goal was, in the words of Catherine Booth, to 'subdue kingdoms' and to 'revolutionize the religious opinions of the country'.[12] In the Irish context the sectarian implications of this supposedly non-partisan religious upheaval would create a whole range of unexpected difficulties for Reynolds and her officers.

GENDER

During the two and a half years that Caroline Reynolds was in charge of the Army's work in Ireland approximately thirty-five women served as corps leaders or as 'second-in-command'. During this time they 'opened' fifteen corps, all based in the North of the country. The social background of the women who served in Ireland reflects the general trends within the Army as a whole.[13] For the most part they were English, and either from substantial Midland towns, such as Nottingham, Cheltenham or Northampton, or from one of the working-class districts of London, such as Whitechapel, Hammersmith or Bethnal Green. Only three of these early officers were Irish women.[14] They are likely to have been among the Army's first converts, coming as they did from Belfast, Lisburn and Newtownards, three of the first four established corps.

Like most Salvation Army officers the women who came to Ireland were predominantly young and single. Of the thirty-five, ages are known for eighteen. One was 17, ten were between 18 and 21, and seven were 22 or older, including a small cluster of four who were aged between 28 and 40. This last group included Caroline Reynolds, who was probably in her late thirties. All but two of the women were single: Mrs Broadhurst from Lisburn was widowed, but Reynolds was married. Unusually, her husband seems to have accompanied her to Ireland, although there is no mention of his involvement in Army activities at any stage. Before joining the Army most of the women had been employed in traditional working-class occupations. Several had been involved in the textile industry, as dressmakers or mill workers; others had worked in the manufacturing sector; and some had been engaged in domestic service. Most of them had had some association with Methodism, even if they had not been regular attenders of religious services. All of them had been converted through the work of the Salvation Army. Thus, a Salvation Army officer in Ireland in the early 1880s was likely to be a young, single woman from the East End of London or the English Midlands who was a member of the 'respectable' working class and had loose connections to Methodism.

When Reynolds and her officers arrived in Belfast they adopted the standard operating procedure for opening a new Salvation Army corps. This was a process that they repeated six times within the next two months, as corps were established in several areas of Belfast along with Londonderry, Newtownards and Lisburn. The opening of Belfast, then, was a model for Army procedure throughout this period. Before the women arrived in the city Reynolds' aide-de-camp, H.D. Edmonds, had made some initial contact with local Christians.[15] This was probably with members of Belfast's Methodist community, several of whom were noted as attending the early meetings. In April 1880 advertisements were placed in local papers and on placards announcing the arrival of the Salvation Army. On the day of their arrival Reynolds and her officers rented lodgings and a small hall for their regular weeknight services.[16]

The Army's basic procedure when beginning a work was to assemble in a public location and conduct an open-air meeting. This involved hymn-singing and loud exhortations to passers-by to attend an indoor service, to be held subsequently in a nearby hall. Once a crowd had gathered the officers would lead a procession through the streets to the hall, where an informal gospel meeting would commence.[17] Opening prayers, Bible readings and musical solos were interspersed with congregational singing, personal testimonies and a gospel message. The culmination of the evening was the call to conversion and time was set aside at the end for 'private conversation' with convinced members of the audience.

These meetings were lively and informal occasions, and the women were responsible for all aspects of their organisation and conduct, including the preaching of the sermon. This was a highly unusual proceeding: the tradition of female preaching in early-nineteenth-century Methodism had declined dramatically by this time, and certainly in Ireland there had been very few women who had ever preached publicly.[18] These public addresses, however, were not the complex expositions of biblical texts that were common practice among contemporary clergymen. Instead they were short exhortations, based more upon personal testimony than on any in-depth knowledge of Scripture, in which sinners were urged to repent of their sins and be saved. As a report in the *Belfast News-Letter* noted:

> The members of the Army at present in Belfast disavow all pretensions of influencing their hearers in the elaborate and carefully prepared form of the pulpit address – in fact, at their meeting last night, judging by their statements they do not appear to regard sermons with much favour. Their addresses are generally brief, and characterised by extreme simplicity, logical sequence, rhetorical effect, and literary ornamentation being entirely wanting, and they consisted largely of details of their own spiritual experiences, narrated in a plain and unattractive manner, and delivered in a somewhat monotonous tone.[19]

When the Salvation Army began its work in Enniskillen in June 1881 the report in the local newspaper, the *Impartial Reporter*, highlighted the informal character of this public preaching:

> Captain Peck sang a verse of 'I'm Praying for You,' to the air of 'Kathleen Mavourneen', and then addressed the meeting. This lady thanked God for the peace she enjoyed. She had once got it and had lost it, and lost it because, as she thought, she had not talked to others about their salvation, but she had got it again and went to the Soldiers' Home and had given herself up to God. She now found that Jesus was with her in trial and tribulation as well as in joy; and she asked any present who had not already done so to give up their all to Jesus.[20]

Peck's intention was not to expound Scripture, but to win the hearts of her listeners through her warmly expressed sentiment and earnest conviction. In doing so she and the other Army women, although clearly acting in a controversial fashion, were not really adopting full ministerial roles. They were, to use a phrase from early Methodism, simply 'exhorting' the people from their own experiences.

That said, Reynolds and her officers were in sole charge of a corps once it had been 'opened' and exercised full authority in its administration. They were responsible for organising the times and places of meetings, and for gathering supporters together to attend. Once a corps was established the women were responsible for the pastoral oversight of new members and for ensuring their ongoing commitment to Army services through events such as 'Hallelujah Free and Easy's or all-night prayer sessions. Phoebe Strong, for example, concerned about the 'discontent and coldness' within her Lisburn corps, held a 'six days' shake up' followed by an 'All Night of Prayer', at which numerous souls were saved.[21]

The responsibility involved in running a corps and in leading open-air services seems all the more impressive when the youth of these women is taken into consideration. For many of these young adults it was their first serious posting and their first time in charge of a corps, and they expressed a whole range of emotions when confronted with the task that lay before them. Many of the women who came to Ireland voiced fears about leaving home, about their parents' disapproval of their actions and about their own inability to cope with the enormous responsibility of corps leadership. Annie Lockwood, who was in command of the Belfast II (Shankill Road) corps, reported that 'my heart sank within me when I saw the water and the great big vessel' that was to take her to Ireland. As she said about being in charge of her own corps, 'I felt the awful responsibility so keenly at times that I could not sleep or eat scarcely and often went to sleep weeping; but stood in the strength of the Lord.'[22]

Other Army women were similarly convinced of their inability to carry out their task in their own strength. Sister Marshall wrote: 'I know I'm weak, but God made a world out of nothing and he can make something of me.'[23] Even Caroline Reynolds expressed her insecurities at taking up the Ireland commission. 'I've had no power but the power of God to hold me up,' she once remarked. 'I have put myself in the hands of God and the General . . . I feel I am nothing, but I feel my flesh is strengthened by His Spirit, and He will work.'[24]

Despite their self-doubt, the certainty of God's support for their actions gave these early Army women the courage and determination to carry on their work, even in the face of difficulty or opposition. Captain Elizabeth Spencer of Lisburn was said to love preaching in the open air, 'for often when the weather was quite unfit, in our

judgement, her voice was heard in the market place and in the streets .
. . shouting the praises of Jesus'.[25] Captain Fysh of Londonderry corps
declared, 'I do like to see the big sailors come rolling out and getting
under the fountain . . . I am determined to fight more than ever and
bring honour and glory to the kingdom of God.'[26] These women's
faith gave them the power to rise above social convention and
personal feelings of inadequacy to do what they felt was God's will.

At first the local response to the arrival of the Salvation Army in
Ireland was quite favourable. In Belfast 'people from all the different
places of worship in the town' attended the early meetings and in
Londonderry there was 'a good attendance of respectable people',
including many from local Protestant churches.[27] In Belfast there was
also a positive response from the poorer classes. According to Reynolds,
'the poorest of the Irish people' were attending the meetings, 'some
with no bonnets, no shoes', and several notorious drunkards had been
converted.[28]

The local newspapers reflected more diverse opinions concerning
the activities of this new religious group. Surprisingly, there were
virtually no critical reviews of these women as public preachers. In
fact they were generally praised for their leadership abilities. The
Derry Journal, a newspaper that was otherwise scathing in its criticism
of Army activities, publicly admired these young women for acting
calmly and standing their ground during a riot.[29] The *Impartial
Reporter*, rather than criticising Caroline Reynolds for preaching in
public, praised her for her 'tact and sweet methods of address'.[30] Local
people also seem to have admired the Army women. According to
one woman from Newtownards, 'Oh, them sisters are doing a lot of
good. They are getting in people who never went anywhere.'[31]

However, the press did express disapproval of the way in which
the women conducted religious services and the style of their delivery.
Thus, Army women were reported as bursting into tears and making
spontaneous outbursts during services, which was clearly considered
to be unseemly behaviour.[32] Commentators were also critical of the
Army's sentimental terminology and military overtones. In a sarcastic
reference to the Army's habit of giving their members nicknames the
Derry Journal joked about the activities of 'Sister More-Than-Good-
Enough' and 'Mother Steal-Them-To-Glory'.[33]

Most commonly, however, local newspapers commented on the
working-class accents and the preaching style of the Army women.

According to the leader writer in the *Belfast Morning News*, 'the destructiveness of [the Army's] oral artillery' was not confined to sin:

> Sin suffered severely, so, some people might think, did religion, but the Queen's English was nowhere in the strife. Unhappy verbs went searching about for the nouns that should have been their nominatives, or, finding them, discovered that they were not the correct thing after all. Bewildered prepositions were hauled in to increase the force of impossible infinitive moods, adjectives found themselves called on to do duty for adverbs who were away qualifying nouns instead of attending to their legitimate duties . . . But most of all we pitied the letter 'h'. Had that unhappy aspirate been the Father of Lies himself, it could scarcely have received a worse reception at the hands of the feminine evangelists (?) [*sic*] It was ruthlessly torn from its proper position in front of words to which it legitimately belonged, and thrust upon parts of speech that knew it not.[34]

To reporters and other middle-class Protestants the Army's actions were 'a travesty of religion and a burlesque of Christianity'.[35] The open-air services, the public processions, the homely music and the personal testimonies were a vulgar display, and lacked the reverence and solemnity that public religious services ought to have.

THE SALVATION ARMY AND IRELAND

Before their arrival in the country the Salvation Army's perception of Ireland and the Irish was the one commonly held by many in Victorian Britain: it was a poor, backward country with an economy based largely on agriculture, and its people were lazy, rebellious and tyrannised by the Catholic Church.[36] Army officers expected Ireland to be 'a miserable mixture of mud cabins, a little whitewash, human beings, pigs, poultry and filth'.[37] Their attitudes towards the Irish were also fairly stereotypical. For Annie Lockwood, they were 'rebellious Irishmen'[38] and according to George Railton, William Booth's second-in-command, the Irish were 'born orators . . . [A]s to the energy and other fighting qualities of the race, there is equally little question . . . To them, religion is a thing never to laugh at, but generally to fight over.'[39]

That the Salvation Army used such stereotypes suggests that, like many other British observers, its members had little or no awareness of the existence of Irish Protestantism, the peculiarities of its denominational divisions or the chronic tensions that characterised its relations with Irish Catholicism. However, this was not the case. The commitment to a non-sectarian approach to evangelism in Ireland was one in which the Army took pride. William Booth had declared that the Army's aim was to battle only 'sinfulism' and its intention was to steer well clear of sectarian rivalry. *All The World*, an Army magazine devoted to foreign missions, later claimed that the Army was ideally placed to 'save Ireland' because 'we have no politics, and therefore cannot enter into discussions or arouse enmity between man and man on that point'.[40] Caroline Reynolds proudly recalled the Army's ignorance of sectarian symbols and images in its preparations for the work in Ireland. She noted that the flag representing the Army's Irish campaign (the 'colours') 'had a green corner with the harp and no crown. We didn't know that the harp without the crown was treason. Then we had orange hymn-books. The Orangemen gloried in that, and the Catholics were wild at it.'[41] Another Army officer, describing the work in Dublin, stated: 'We always can get crowds of all kinds to come an' hear us, because we're not proselytisers and don't want to dhraw thim from their own places of worship, in fact it's the people who go nowhere we want.'[42] The Salvation Army was determined to operate as a neutral evangelising force.

While these may have been noble sentiments, it soon became evident that, despite its protestations to the contrary, the Army had allied itself with the Protestant community. First of all, of the fifteen corps established under Reynolds' command all were based in the North, most were clustered in the Northeast, the region with the greatest concentration of Protestants, and only four were located outside Counties Antrim, Down and Armagh. It was not until 1888 that the first corps outside the province of Ulster was established, and even then it was located in Rathmines, a largely Protestant suburb of Dublin.[43]

Secondly, it was clear from the outset that most of the Army's support was drawn from the ranks of the various Irish Protestant denominations. This was not surprising. All shared a basic commitment to evangelical theology, and a general agreement about the value of evangelisation and open-air mission work. Irish Methodists were particularly supportive. As a denomination Methodism had pioneered the practice of outdoor evangelism and open-air revivals. Booth's Methodist background and his adaptation of traditional Methodist forms for the Army gave the two denominations a natural affinity. Irish Methodist ministers spoke at Army services, allowed the Army to use their churches, and publicly defended its methods and approach.[44] Presbyterians, however, had embraced such evangelistic techniques only in recent decades, while the Church of Ireland, although by this stage a predominantly evangelical body, still maintained a greater emphasis on religious propriety and the importance of the parish. At times both denominations could be deeply suspicious of the populist methods so enthusiastically pursued by the Salvation Army and its Methodist supporters.

Thirdly, the affiliation of the Salvation Army with Irish Protestantism was heightened by its occupation of overtly Protestant spaces, such as Orange halls, and its adoption of overtly Protestant metaphors and historical images. For example, reports from Army officers in Londonderry routinely compared their work in the city to the siege of 1688. The headlines for one article in the *War Cry* screamed: 'IRELAND – LONDONDERRY – 1688 contrasted with 1880 – Hosts of Hell camped around – The Army continues victorious – Captain Strong fired at – . . . The Work telling on the people', and the article itself went on to state:

> On Thursday, 12th August there were celebrations here in commemoration of the **Opening of the City Gates** after the memorable siege lasting from the 13th December previous, nearly 200 years ago. Great as was this victory over **A Treacherous Enemy** and securing, as it did, to the whole nation, **Civil and Religious Liberty**, a still greater victory has been achieved over the Arch-Enemy of Souls since the Salvation Army first stormed the heights of sin in this same city, nearly three months ago, securing, as it did, in the hands of the Lord, Spiritual Liberty . . . [45]

A report in the following year declared:

> We have just concluded a seven days' siege of Beelzebub's fortresses in Londonderry, with no small success . . . All we can say to those who are still pushing the battle before the walls is,

let your motto be 'No Surrender,' continue to shout hallelujah and let your rams' horns be blown in every street, and the walls of sin soon will totter and fall, for not all the booms, walls or armies of Hell can stay the King's approach.[46]

By making this comparison the Army reflected its basic empathy with the ideals of the beseiged, even if it was trying to suggest a spiritual alternative.

The object of the Army's activities confirmed what their use of Protestant buildings and metaphors only suggested. Although the Army women in Ireland were keen to convert anyone who, in their view, was in need of the gospel, it was clear that they viewed Catholics as particularly needful of salvation.[47] Caroline Reynolds described the ruffians who opposed her Londonderry services as 'regular Fenians' and 'a beautiful lot of people to get saved!'[48] Later she deliberately targeted Londonderry's Catholics by timing her open-air meetings to coincide with the end of Sunday Mass.[49] Despite the ongoing resistance of Irish Catholics to conversion, the Army remained committed to a policy of expansion into the South and West of the country. As Captain Ellen Daly reported on her efforts in Maryborough, County Laois: 'There are twenty times as many Roman Catholics as there are Protestants in the town, and the former are forbidden by their priests to enter our hall, therefore our work progresses but slowly.'[50]

Despite its best intentions, the Army appeared to be firmly 'Protestant' in its sympathies and intent. For the women leading the campaign in Ireland this had some unexpected consequences. While Caroline Reynolds and her fellow officers were prepared for opposition, and even relished it as a sign of their effectiveness, they were not ready for their activities to become almost entirely subsumed into a pre-existing set of sectarian and interdenominational rivalries. The most dramatic instances of this local takeover occurred in Londonderry and Enniskillen.

Caroline Reynolds, along with Elizabeth Spencer and Polly Flinn, began work in Londonderry on 1 June 1880. They hired a skating rink on the Strand Road, and began holding regular open-air and indoor meetings. Within days their processions were attracting hostile crowds and local police constables had been called to ensure the women's safety. By the beginning of August local supporters of the

Army, described in the local press as Protestants, had formed themselves into a 'bodyguard' to protect the procession from what was
now a much more aggressive mob. Inevitably this led to arrests and
appearances before local magistrates, generally on the charge of
obstructing the thoroughfare. After a period of relative calm a massive
riot ensued in April 1881. At the subsequent petty sessions the Mayor
made it clear that, although he was willing to protect the Army inside
the hall, he was not prepared to use the police to protect members on
the streets. The implications of this decision for the safety of the
Army's processions were left unrealised because popular violence
against the Army subsided, and processions and meetings were no
longer disturbed.[51]

A similar sort of opposition was encountered when Caroline
Reynolds, accompanied by Captains Sarah Broadhurst, Annie Parke
and Martha Reid, began work in Enniskillen in early March 1881.[52]
Here the situation was complicated by the fact that a rival organisation, the Hallelujah Army, had already booked the Town Hall and
had commenced outdoor evangelistic services.[53] The Salvation Army
then hired the Protestant Hall, situated at the far eastern end of the
town. Both organizations were now holding nightly open-air services
and processing through the streets. As in Londonderry, this behaviour
soon attracted a hostile mob. Both Armies acquired local 'bodyguards'
and the police were frequently called out to maintain order. In
Enniskillen, however, the magistrates were ill-prepared for such
violence and on Saturday 2 April they 'proclaimed' the town: until
further notice all public assemblies that might provoke a breach of the
peace would be dispersed and participants who refused to go quietly
would be arrested. Twenty extra police officers were called up for
emergency duty.

EXPLANATIONS

At the most basic level the violence directed towards the Salvation
Army in these two towns can be seen as a manifestation of working-
class opposition to the Army's attempts to invade its neighbourhoods
and transform its culture. Local newspapers regularly described the
crowds who disrupted Army processions as 'mobs of low rowdies',
'boys and girls shouting and cheering', a 'crowd of roughs and girls',

and 'lawless mobs of ill-disposed roughs and ragamuffins'.[54] The behaviour exhibited by these crowds also suggests a class interpretation. Irish crowds 'jostled, groaned and hissed' at the Army women as they processed the streets. They hooted and jeered at them, and occasionally beat them with sticks or pelted them with mud and rotten eggs. In Enniskillen crowds of local people even organised themselves into an alternative army, conducting rival processions, carrying home-made banners and singing irreverent songs.[55] All this was behaviour that the Army had encountered in England.[56] The primary intention was not actual physical harm, nor was it an attack on the Army's Protestantism. It was clearly designed to mock the efforts of the Army women and subject them to ritual forms of humiliation. It was a traditional response from within working-class communities to the aggressive methods that the Army had adopted.

That said, the inhabitants of both Londonderry and Enniskillen saw this violence in rather more local terms. In Londonderry public opinion, in the form of comment in and letters to local newspapers, and the pronouncements of magistrates, clearly perceived the violence surrounding the Army as a clash between its Protestant supporters and Catholic mobs. The *Derry Sentinel*, the voice of the Londonderry Protestant community, was adamant that it was 'Bogside rowdies' who had led these 'disgraceful' and 'outrageous' attacks on the Army women. According to one correspondent, 'there is no doubt but the disturbance is created by the lower order of the Roman Catholics'.[57] Another interpreted this opposition as an example of the 'bigoted and intolerant' nature of Irish Catholicism, a denomination inherently opposed to 'the preaching of God's Word'.[58] For Londonderry's Protestants, then, the action of the Catholic mob was not a form of working-class hostility but religious persecution. It was seen as a violation of the rights of free assembly, free speech and religious expression.[59] Magistrates and police, therefore, had a duty to 'curb the bigotry and lawlessness which now disgraces Derry',[60] and in doing so to uphold these freedoms.

For the *Derry Journal*, the *Sentinel's* main rival, representing the views of Londonderry's Catholic community, the violence surrounding the Army's processions was clearly caused by their own actions and the behaviour of their Protestant 'bodyguard'. The Army's activities were an obvious public nuisance and an 'opportunity for rowdies to throw stones or shout the war-cry of "No Surrender" under cover of accompanying the "Army"'.[61] If 'the conduct of the "Salvationists" directly or indirectly leads to serious breaches of the peace', then the logical conclusion was 'for those entrusted with the preservation of life and property to use their powers in such a way as that peace and security shall be enjoyed'.[62] For the *Journal* this meant that magistrates should prevent public processions from taking place, or at least prohibit the Army from singing in the streets. By voicing this desire for public order the *Journal* was not expressing its opposition to the Salvation Army as a religious organisation. Indeed, it openly absolved the Army from any responsibility for the violence surrounding its meetings.[63] Neither was it attacking the Protestant religion or the civil and religious liberties that the *Sentinel* held so dear. For the *Journal* the issue at stake was much more pragmatic: 'Freedom of preachment and practice is all very well in its way, but when that freedom degenerates into a nuisance, and becomes a shield for displays of intolerance and rowdyism, it is the duty of every right-thinking man to set his face against it.'[64] Regardless of the crowd's exact motives, public opinion in Londonderry readily interpreted their hostility towards Army activity in sectarian terms.

In Enniskillen the response of the inhabitants to the arrival of the Salvation Army was rather different, although the town had an equally large working-class population and this community expressed considerable hostility towards the Army's public efforts. Local Protestants did not argue that it was Catholic mobs attacking Protestant processions, nor did Catholics publicly object to the disruption caused. In fact the violence against the Army was not really an issue. What was significant was the way in which one section of the local elite handled this violence and how that was interpreted by their denominational rivals.

Enniskillen's local elite was controlled by Protestants. Members of the Church of Ireland, while comprising only 36 per cent of the population, occupied most of the local government positions and, in particular, the magistracy.[65] Methodists, while only 4 per cent of the population, were clearly an affluent and influential part of the town elite.[66] They had built a grand church on the main street[67] and comprised about one third of the Town Commission.[68] Despite the similarities between the various Protestant groupings, numerous tensions simmered below the surface.

When the Salvation Army arrived in Enniskillen and began conducting evangelistic meetings local Methodists were their obvious supporters.[69] When magistrates decided to proclaim the town Methodists were obviously concerned and the next day their minister, the Reverend William Quarry, conducted an open-air service as a form of protest. The audience consisted of the leading members of the town's Methodist community, including professionals, businessmen and a number of town commissioners. The magistrates, who were determined to enforce their ruling, asked the police to disperse the crowd. In the process 'one or two persons were rather roughly handled' and a party of soldiers from the nearby garrison was called out. It arrived, allegedly, with bayonets fixed, but by that time the meeting had already ended.

These events became the major point of contention between local magistrates and the Methodist community. Enniskillen's magistrates argued that proclamation was essential. The police force was currently under strength and constables were exhausted from their now-nightly duty of protecting the various processions. This level of policing was expensive and would force an increase in the local rates. The only way to guarantee tranquillity was to prevent all assemblies.

To those 'respectable' Methodists who had attended Quarry's meeting, however, the proclamation looked like a serious threat to religious freedom, if not quite an overt attack on local Methodism. At an 'indignation meeting' held in the Methodist schoolroom the following day leading members of the Methodist community delivered their opinion that Enniskillen's Anglican magistrates were determined to prevent them from practising their religion in their own way. According to one speaker, the soldiers were summoned simply because Methodists had 'an open Bible' in a public place. S.B. Humphreys, manager of the Sligo Railway Company and a leading Methodist layman, declared that this was the first time in Ireland that 'a public prayer meeting was a breach of the law'. Soon other eminent Methodists were translating their fears for the future of Methodism in Enniskillen into a concern for 'civil and religious liberty' in general. A number of contributors made it clear that this was not a quarrel with Catholicism: Rev. Quarry made it plain that '[t]heir controversy was not with Roman Catholics and the Roman Catholic had yet to be found who had insulted him . . . The police were the disturbing element, and the controversy was between the respectable people of Enniskillen and the authorities.' Mr Jeremiah Jordan, MP for South Fermanagh and a Methodist, also protested, arguing that men, generally of one class and denomination, appointed for political service by certain magnates could have as little sympathy with dissent as with the common people.

The anger within Enniskillen's Methodist community over their treatment (and indirectly, the treatment of the Salvation Army) was, to a certain extent understandable. Although confronted with similar public disorder decisions, no other Irish magistrates had felt the need to proclaim their towns because of the Army's presence. Town commissioners who had sought a compromise found that magistrates had gone ahead without any further consultation. Stung by this exclusion from the local decision-making process, Methodists petitioned the Chief Secretary and demanded the resident magistrate's resignation.[70] In response magistrates summonsed nine leading townsmen (five of whom were Methodists) on a charge of obstruction. Although the charge was eventually dropped and the resident magistrate remained in his post, relations between the two groups had reached a low ebb.[71]

In both Londonderry and Enniskillen the female officers of the Salvation Army found themselves caught up in local conflicts that they had not expected. They were prepared for traditional working-class opposition; what they had not anticipated was the way in which this opposition would be interpreted. They had not expected the violence against their processions in Londonderry to be seen as a case of Catholics against Protestants, nor did they expect that their activities in Enniskillen would provoke a major confrontation between Anglicans and Dissenters. In both cases the Army found itself the largely unwitting catalyst in a local confrontation that had little to do with either its methods or its message.

CONCLUSION

One aspect of the public disorder surrounding the Salvation Army's campaigns in Londonderry and Enniskillen that has been neglected so far is the issue of gender. After all, it was women such as Caroline Reynolds, Polly Flinn and Sarah Broadhurst who were in charge of the Army's work in these two towns, and were on the front lines of the violence and controversy. How did local communities in the North of Ireland respond to the presence of women leading public processions and conducting religious services? Surprisingly, public criticism on these grounds is virtually non-existent. However, all shades of public opinion, regardless of their attitude to the Army in general, reflected traditional notions about the treatment of women and agreed that any violence against females was particularly disgraceful. As the *Sentinal* stated: 'We blush at the idea that the Maiden City contains people capable of bringing disgrace upon our common Christianity and on the gallantry to the fair sex for which Irishmen are proverbial.'[72] Those who did attack Army women were deemed 'cowards' who had clearly forgotten 'their manhood and their manners'.[73] Others felt that, because the Army's activities consisted of just 'a few ladies singing', it was impossible for them to pose a serious threat to local inhabitants or their interests. To oppose their activities, therefore, was to overreact to them.

The Salvation Army women who began the work in Ireland had been prepared for violence, but they were blithely, and perhaps naively, unaware of the possible sectarian implications of their work. That said, they braved the mobs with a remarkable sense of determination. The obstacles which they encountered and their achievement were epitomised in this account of Mrs Broadhurst, a leader in Enniskillen:

> In the face of the howling mob, and contrary to the wishes of the authorities, and, indeed, we might say of many professing Christians . . . she unfurled the banner of the glorious Gospel in the streets of Enniskillen . . . Her unflinching pursuit of the glorious work, and her anxiety to go wherever she thought good might be done for her Lord and Master, has gained her the esteem and affection of, I might say, every soldier and friend of the Army here.[74]

'WOMEN'S WORK FOR WOMEN': THE IRISH PRESBYTERIAN ZENANA MISSION, 1874–1914

Myrtle Hill

Women's Work was the title of the quarterly magazine of the Female Association in Connection with the Foreign Missions of the Presbyterian Church in Ireland.[1] Popularly known as the 'Zenana' Mission, this association was founded in 1874 to recruit and support female teachers and medical workers for the purpose of 'promoting Christianity among the women of the East'. The aim of this essay is to examine the opportunities the mission provided for both voluntary and salaried work, at home and abroad, for a small group of women in late nineteenth- and early twentieth-century Ireland.

The official records of the mission provide us with a fairly clear picture of a vast organisational enterprise stretching from Ireland to the Near East. The wealth of factual details on income and expenditure, on the setting up of schools, dispensaries and hospitals, and on the movements of the missionaries in India and China facilitate our understanding of the 'business' of missions: how they were funded, organised, marketed both at home and abroad; about those who staffed the mission office in Belfast; and the arrangements for recruitment, training and support of the missionaries themselves. More subjective information, on attitudes, experiences or achievements, is not so readily accessible, and research into such areas necessitates a more cautious approach and sensitive analysis of the materials, whether these be the letters, diaries and biographies of individuals, or missionary magazines and reports. Superimposed on the gender bias of male writers and spokesmen are the barriers created by religious discourse, where the language itself and the wealth of images employed often obscure the reality of individual experience. Moreover, the writings of the women who embraced this tradition were directed at a particular type of readership. They were meant to encourage and inspire, and are thus more often reflections of faith than expressions of individuals. The task of the historian is to locate the words and actions of such women firmly in their context, to recognise the complex interlacing strands that determined the lifestyle and belief system of individuals who were themselves of different age, background and personality types. It is also important to note that, while the impact of the cultural imperialism within which much missionary work was carried out lies outside the remit of this particular paper, the voices of the indigenous women of the East were silenced throughout this missionary discourse.[2]

There was, of course, already a well-established tradition of women working in the foreign mission field. From the early nineteenth century the wives of male missionaries had played crucial roles in sustaining the missionary enterprise. Mission boards considered it important that their male agents married before taking up their posts in foreign communities and alien cultures.[3] Not only would this reduce the likelihood of unsuitable liaisons and possible scandals, but the right type of partner would be a valuable addition to the mission work.[4] Indeed, it is clear that the many women who accompanied their husbands to foreign fields not only supported them in their work, by replicating the comforts of western family life, but used their own skills and experiences in supervising schools, looking after orphans, reading Bible stories and so forth.[5] However, despite frequent acknowledgement of their contributions in the pages of both *Women's Work* and the male Foreign Mission's *Missionary Herald*, these women had no independent status. As in secular society generally, the partnerships were far from equal and women's work was viewed as voluntary, to be fitted around family life, which, it was often noted, severely restricted their opportunities. Indeed, family life was not easy to sustain in the mission field, with deaths of infants regularly reported and mothers enduring lengthy separation from their older children, who were sent back to Ireland or England for schooling.[6] Moreover, although many missionary wives had their own sense of religious vocation, they had no choice but to return home on the death or retirement of their husbands.[7]

The decision to engage single women for the specific purpose of missionary work seems to have been influenced by the examples of American women and of deaconess work in Germany. While it was stated that women were primarily needed to minister to the wives and daughters of converts,[8] the new concern to educate women also reflected the failure, in general terms, of the foreign mission in converting Indian men.[9] In India, as in Ireland, women were regarded as both obstacles to, and agents for, change.[10] At both the first and second annual general meetings of the Female Association experienced male missionaries stressed that 'evangelise men as you may – the reformation will not become national till the women are saved too'.[11] Only other women, unencumbered by family responsibilities and dedicated to the task, could, it was argued, penetrate the cultural isolation of the Indian female, who was most frequently represented as an 'idle, helpless prisoner' in need of moral rescue.[12] This was the basis of the appeal to the women of Ireland's Presbyterian community, first made at a meeting in Belfast organised by William Fleming Stevenson, Convenor of the Church's Foreign Mission. The response of local 'ladies' to impassioned speeches from a veteran missionary and an Indian 'convert from heathenism' was immediate and whole-hearted.[13] As Maria Luddy has pointed out, in their involvement in foreign missionary work women were merely 'bringing to foreign parts that religious message which their fund-raisers and supporters already saw in action, though on a different scale, in Ireland'.[14] By 1914 the Female Association had sent a total of 101 Irishwomen to India or China. While in the field these 'Zenana' agents worked under the guidance of male missionaries and, technically at least, were controlled by the church's Board of Missions, the ethos, direction and success of the operation were largely determined by the work, contributions, support and commitment of women.

A strong and efficient home base was clearly essential for the smooth running of the operation and critical to the success of the entire enterprise. That this was achieved with such remarkable speed was a reflection of the already intensive nature of women's involvement in church work.[15] The first annual general report indicates that the association drew its strength from the middle-class Presbyterian communities, not only of Belfast and the North-east, but also of southern centres such as Cork, Limerick and Dublin. A team of dedicated women filled the organisational and administrative posts: fifty-eight women served on the General Committee; three secretaries and a treasurer (all of them female) were responsible for much of the day-to-day work; while an examining committee of two women and three men assessed the credentials of candidates for the missionary field. The association could also avail of the expertise of an all-male Consulting Committee of fourteen ministers.[16]

The energy, skills and talent of individual women were used on behalf of the mission through a network linking them with the central administration. Members paid a minimum of one shilling per annum; those paying ten guineas became life members; congregational auxiliaries (of which forty-nine were reported at the first meeting) could be formed by any interested woman in the church; and district branches (fourteen formed in the first year) brought these groups together.[17] William Addley, in his thesis on the Irish Presbyterian foreign missions, sees this Zenana structure as a particularly important innovation. He argues that, by focusing on individual rather than congregational membership, this association developed a new concept of mission support, and fostered a special relationship between church and mission: where the male Foreign Mission belonged to, and was made up of, the whole church, the Zenana was a distinctive group within the church, which aimed to ensure that every girl and woman connected to the congregation should contribute to its work. It was thus particularly successful in stimulating personal interest and commitment, harnessing the energies and talents and targeting the sympathies of individual women.[18]

Women's expertise in budgetary matters has frequently been noted by historians and the workings of this association also testify to the 'power of the purse'.[19] Membership subscriptions were collected by volunteers, whose job was to canvas the congregation, and no doubt the lack of anonymity in these arrangements was a persuasive factor. Income also came from donations, by individuals or groups, for general or specific purposes. For example, the first annual report indicates that out of an income of £1,201.9.3, £450 came from one donor. In that same year two 'fellow workers' also undertook responsibility for the costs of the training, outfitting and passage, and one year's salary, of the first female medical missionary.[20] Personal links between members of a congregation and those in the mission field often ensured a particularly high level of commitment to the cause. Gillian McClelland, for example, highlights the proportionally significant financial contributions made to the Zenana by Fisherwick Church's Working Women's Association, several of whose members served abroad. While the missionaries themselves maintained close contact with the home base, their mothers, other relatives and friends energetically campaigned and collected on their behalf.[21]

Indeed, a clear picture emerges from this study of a close-knit community of women, linked through congregational loyalty or extended family membership, embracing a dynamic religious culture that to a large extent shaped their outlook and determined their actions. Although the part played by Presbyterian middle-class men in the industrial and cultural development of the North-east of Ireland has been well-documented, the activities and experience of women of this class are only now receiving the attention they deserve. During a period when 'the church absorbed women's physical and intellectual energy in a way no other institution did',[22] class and gender interacted to produce a vibrant network of activists. In congregations such as Fisherwick Church or Fitzroy Avenue[23] the wives and daughters of businessmen and merchants contributed their time, money and education to what they regarded as the moral imperative of sharing 'the light of life' with their 'dark' sisters in the East.[24]

Most of those involved in the administrative work of the mission appear to have had close associations with the church from childhood. Their spiritual lives had been nurtured in Sunday school and Bible classes, they expressed a strong sense of religious vocation, and many were themselves daughters of the manse or related to missionaries. The life of Mary Crawford Brown is a good example of those who answered the call 'to be something for Him, to do something for Him' through service at home.[25] Her paternal and maternal grandparents had been missionaries, and when her own aspiration to follow in their footsteps was thwarted by ill health she dedicated herself to supporting the mission from her home base.[26] Becoming the editor of the newly named *Women's Work* in 1890, Mary Brown served in this capacity for twenty-eight years, during which time the circulation rose dramatically.[27] Those who served as secretaries were also either married or otherwise related to ministers or missionaries and the early history of the mission testifies to the extent of their dedication. For example, the average length of service for the first six secretaries to the association (two recording secretaries, two home corresponding secretaries and two foreign corresponding secretaries) was seventeen years.[28] Mrs Park was recording secretary for thirty-four years, while the treasurer, Mrs Lemon, remained in post for thirty-five years, devoting every morning to the task of receiving subscriptions, paying missionaries' salaries and expenses, and preparing and presenting annual statements.[29] By the time she gave up her post the Zenana budget had grown so large that it was put under the control of the Financial Secretary of the Church.[30]

This intensive commitment had significant implications for the financial as well as the administrative success of the enterprise, for, with women acting as unpaid managers, secretaries, treasurers, collectors and organisers, much of the essential day-to-day work was carried out at no cost to the mission. The financial outlay at home was thus kept to a minimum; the costs of running the office – postage and printing, room hire, hosting events, travel and other expenses – amounted to between only three and twelve per cent of the overall expenditure.[31] The leadership, encouragement and example of such women also generated a high level of enthusiasm for fund-raising activities in congregational auxiliaries and women's associations throughout Ireland. Money was raised at bazaars, through penny-a-month envelopes, and by the sale of the eggs of missionary hens, the honey of missionary bees or the items made in sewing circles blessed by prayer.[32] Women also donated a range of other gifts – including toys, books, pianos and clothes – for use in Zenana homes, orphanages, schools or hospitals.[33] Only three years after its formation it was noted that Zenana auxiliaries were contributing two or three times as much as the congregations they represented had given to the church's foreign mission.[34] Although the financial strength of the mission was subject to fluctuations, a combination of wise investment and sustained fundraising meant that by 1914 the annual income amounted to more than 14,000 pounds.[35]

The importance of missionary literature as a tool 'to edify, loosen purse-strings and to promote recruitment' was recognised from an early stage[36], and it is perhaps relevant that enthusiasm for Zenana literature appears to have surpassed that for the male-run body's publications. In 1899 the *Missionary Herald* lamented its own circulation of 4,000, noting that *Daybreak*[37] needed a grant to keep it going, while *Women's Work* apparently progressed in leaps and bounds, with more than 2,000 new subscriptions a year.[38] It is not difficult to account for the appeal of this publication. Like the *Missionary Herald*, *Women's Work* contained detailed reports of the state of the mission stations, pleas for funding and personnel, and accounts of missionary movements, but it was both lighter in tone and more intimate in its appeal. Clearly targeting a wider readership, its contents included biographies, maps, poems, quizzes and songs. Letters and articles from serving missionaries were of course the mainstay of the work, and served to highlight the mutually dependent relationship between missionaries in the field and their counterparts in the church at home.[39] This bond was strengthened by organisations such as the Missionary Prayer Union, formed in 1885, which all members of auxiliaries were invited to join, 'to remember in prayer our missionaries and their work every Saturday evening'. Members were issued with cards bearing the names of missionaries and giving information on the various mission stations, thus ensuring that prayers offered were both specific and personal.[40] Apart from the spiritual dimension to these activities, they had the effect of more closely involving those at home with the progress of the work abroad, promoting a sense of responsibility for both successes and failures.

On a more practical level, writers in *Women's Work* urged readers to use the 'great deal of local talent waiting to be discovered and developed'; they were encouraged, for example, to 'prepare and read papers dealing with special departments of our mission work, followed by discussion or questions from all present'.[41] Those who served on the executive committee were expected to play a more prominent public role, addressing large gatherings on occasions such as the annual general meetings, which from 1888 preceded the deliberations of the General Assembly of the Presbyterian Church and regularly attracted many hundreds more women than the venue could accommodate.[42] Office-bearers were frequently required to travel and to represent the Irish Zenana at international forums.[43] Although some found this level of public activism 'unwomanly', Mary Brown vigorously asserted the need for women to embrace opportunities to speak from public platforms, arguing that when she did so she was the 'channel of a power not her own' and that it was impossible 'to be enthusiastically silent'.[44]

Although a few leading women did take up the increased opportunities for travel and public speaking, the religious nature of their work, and the fact that it took place in an all-female forum, ensured that it was perceived as enhancing rather than denying traditional womanly virtues. Indeed, in the context of secular calls for women's suffrage, churchmen regarded 'bringing their sisters to Christ' as 'the highest right of Christian women'.[45] However, the fact that much of the work carried out at the home base could be regarded as fairly traditional 'women's work' – voluntary, supportive and 'background' – does not diminish their considerable achievement. With women supporting each other through prayer meetings, sewing circles and fundraising, home mission work opened new possibilities for female assertion inside and outside the home. In a venture that took them out of the private sphere, to become part of a more public campaign to reform the world, many of these women enhanced their personal standing in their families, their congregations and the wider religious culture in which they operated.

For those who carried the message to foreign fields there was more potential to challenge gendered expectations of what constituted appropriate female behaviour, although, as we shall see, both the women themselves and their male counterparts consistently resisted such an interpretation of their activities. Indeed, the fact that extensive travel, difficult cultural adjustments, intellectual and professional training, and a satisfying career, independent of husbands or families, could be grafted on to the traditional model of femininity without fundamentally altering the dominant ideological concept of womanhood, highlights the importance of language, imagery and symbolism in perpetuating conventional gender roles. Male religious leaders, for example, preserved traditional gender differences by stressing that women's aptitude for missionary work was based on what were perceived as the major defining features of femininity:[46] 'submission, love, tenderness, self-sacrifice, devotement, sympathy, are characteristic features of the piety of women, and when joined with gifts, knowledge and grace, they make a model missionary'.[47]

The notions of 'service' and sacrifice are certainly evident in the records left by Zenana missionaries, and the motto printed on *Women's Work* – 'she hath done what she could' – reinforced this impression of their contribution to the mission. Like their counterparts working on the home base, a majority of this early generation of missionary women appear to have been middle-class[48], the daughters of ministers, doctors or businessmen. It is likely, therefore, that the 'devotional domesticity' of middle-class Victorian family life was an important factor in inculcating the sense of duty, mission and purpose that characterised missionary candidates. Many missionary women had entered into evangelical and charitable work at a local level, and at an early age, before venturing into foreign parts. Dr Margaret McNeill, for example, had become a Sunday School teacher at the age of thirteen; Dr Mary McGeorge, daughter of a justice of the peace, had also established an evening Sunday School and regularly visited the sick in her area; others took part in evangelistic work among Belfast mill girls. Many, including Susan Brown, the first woman sent to India by the Presbyterian Female Association, drew inspiration from, and followed the example of, missionary fathers, brothers or other male relatives.[49]

Educational experience also seems to have been influential. The two most prestigious girls' colleges in Ireland, Alexandra College, Dublin, and Victoria College, Belfast, not only provided their middle-class pupils with a sound academic education, but also instilled in them a set of values and a moral code that fitted them well for work of a religious nature. Both colleges subsidised the daughters of ministers or missionaries[50] and developed close links with personnel in the foreign mission stations.[51] Family, school and church life thus combined to intensify the messages of middle-class evangelical Christianity, with its stress on moral behaviour and social justice.

The benefits of new female middle-class educational opportunities were warmly welcomed by the mission leaders of the late nineteenth century. The demands of the mission field had changed from the mid-century, when those denominations that did send out women felt that 'a pious, kind, active, well-formed, patient motherly body, who can cut out and teach needlework, keep house, manage servants and maintain neatness and order, is far more likely to be happy than a young lady with modern accomplishments'.[52] Now women were required in a more professional capacity, as teachers and medical workers, although even this work was perceived as a tool in the primary task of evangelisation.[53] By the early twentieth century the mission was specifically targeting the growing number of female university graduates, whose academic training was regarded as a sound basis for the demands and trials of the mission field:

> Not only because of the knowledge thus gained, but quite as much because her idea of life is widened and deepened. All sorts and conditions of people are met at college. One is taught self-control, self-reliance, humility, sympathy with the view of others [and] *esprit de corps*. Unselfishness and helpfulness are also encouraged. This moral part of university education is as important as a degree, when in the mission field one will have to live months and years perhaps, with fellow-workers of widely different temperaments.[54]

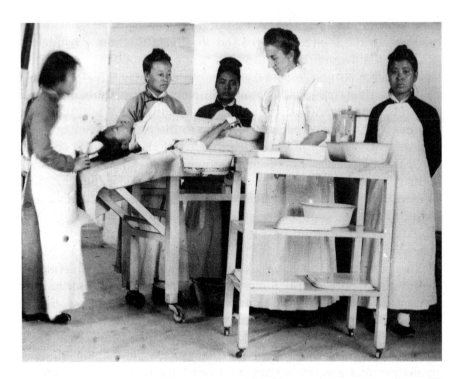

16. A woman missionary doctor, assisted by Chinese nursing attendants, 22
November 1913. Based at Kwanatunky, China, this hospital was part of the
Irish Presbyterian Mission overseas. (Hogg Collection, Ulster Museum,
Belfast. Photograph reproduced with the kind permission of the Trustees of
the National Museums & Galleries of Northern Ireland).

The upholding of moral and specifically female virtues over intellectual achievement is, of course, in keeping with contemporary
religious discourse. In 1892 the founding of a Student Volunteer
Missionary Union established a body of potential recruits, young
women who pledged their 'purpose, if God permits, to become a
foreign missionary'.[55] In 1910 the World Missionary Conference held
in Edinburgh claimed that those who volunteered and did not reach
the field for reasons other than physical fitness numbered no more
that seven per cent of the whole.[56]

The attraction of the mission field for such women was heightened
by the fact that there were few professional openings for the
increasing number of educated middle-class women in Ireland.

Alison Jordan has pointed out that poor pay and lack of security for teachers in local girls' colleges led to a 'steady exodus of highly qualified Irishwomen across the Irish Sea to take up better paid posts in England',[57] while gender bias frequently frustrated those qualifying as doctors in their search for employment.[58] In these circumstances female missionary work assumed a new significance as a full-time professional career, especially relevant to those of a particular class and culture.

Apart from a sense of personal fulfilment, which was an important element of such work, Zenana missionaries received the most up-to-date training and had excellent prospects for professional advancement; many also enjoyed a degree of autonomy in their work that would not have been possible in Ireland. Teachers, for example, were trained in the most progressive 'kindergarten' methods and a considerable proportion of them took up positions as school superintendents in India or China. While the salaries of women were about half of those paid to men, they compared well with earning potential at home and a pension scheme was introduced in the early years of the twentieth century.[59] Female doctors were particularly encouraged and were also offered a wider scope for their skills, a trend that was noted in all the major Protestant female missionary associations and caused one Methodist missionary to comment ironically: 'how strange that the call to our women to advance in medical science and in the study of theology, and then to travel thousands of miles alone, and to live alone in a foreign land, should come from the intensely feminine women of the East'.[60]

The need for medical workers was especially felt in China and by 1908 five of the eight women sent by this mission to Manchuria were doctors. Although the sample is small, the high proportion of women doctors serving in the Zenana mission compared to those following the profession in Ireland (only thirty-three in 1911), and, indeed, compared to the numbers of Irish Presbyterian male missionary doctors sent to India and China[61], suggests that the missionary enterprise provided an important outlet for a new generation of highly qualified women.

However, individual personality traits and social or economic circumstances combine with other factors to render it virtually impossible to disentangle the religious and secular motivations of these women. As already indicated, by the beginning of the First

World War missionary service in mainstream Protestant traditions was becoming more of a profession than a calling, with the divine origin of the missionary impulse coming to be seen as less important than other, more easily identifiable qualifications.[62] An article in *Women's Work* in October 1911 urged a straightforward approach to the question of suitability:

> What is this call? (1) Do you love the Lord Jesus and are you willing to obey him? (2) Have you good health? (3) Have you any duties at home that would prevent you (let us say) from marrying a suitable man? If you can answer all these questions (except the last) in the affirmative, then you have no need to wait for a call – you have the command 'Go'.[63]

As Stuart Piggin has pointed out, the traditional boundaries between the spiritual and the secular perhaps need to be redrawn, 'because frequently secular motives were spiritualised, while spiritual motives were often emptied of altruism'.[64] This seems particularly applicable to the teaching and medical work of this first generation of female missionaries, many of whom regarded respectability, education, teaching, healing and, in particular, the progress of women as trademarks of civilisation, arising from and reliant upon, Christian faith. Their desire to share the privileges of the great nation to which they belonged with the women of India and China inevitably led to a range of paradoxes and tensions in their relationships with indigenous cultures (this will be a central focus of future research). That some could afford and were willing to serve in a voluntary capacity highlights the strong moral imperative that underlaid their activities, but should not detract from either the influence or the impact of more secular aspects of their work.[65]

However, neither academic qualifications nor a sense of vocation were themselves considered a sufficient foundation for missionary work. All recruits, even those professionally trained as nurses, teachers or doctors, also had to undergo specific training before being sent abroad. Several Zenana missionaries, for example, were sent to a deaconesses' training school in Scotland, where their course consisted of training in educational methods, writing reports and keeping accounts as well as Bible study.[66] Care was also taken to foster and develop the devotional life of the students, particularly important as missionary leaders constantly expressed concern about what they regarded as women's inherent weaknesses, both physical and spiritual.[67] Having completed a course along these lines, missionaries new to the field spent the first few months learning the relevant language, in which their expertise was regularly examined, before finally commencing work in orphanage, dispensary, school or hospital.

In the first years of the new mission Zenana agents needed to be flexible enough to adapt to the particular needs of mission stations. For example, although both Miss Forrest and Miss Patteson had been specifically trained for medical work, in fact they spent much of their time at Surat assisting Susan Brown in the mission schools.[68] This 'professional' aspect of work was combined with establishing and teaching in Sunday Schools for girls, evangelising among women in outlying villages, and training local women to be teaching or dispensary assistants.

Missionaries in the field inevitably belonged to tight and exclusive social circles, sustained by faith in the validity of their work, their days enlivened by tennis matches, Christian weddings and missionary conferences. The locations were, of course, exotic, and the working year was broken up by vacations in the mountains in the heat, Christmas in the sunshine and the trials of the rainy season.[69] Yet, while letters home usually reflected ardent devotion to the task in hand, missionaries were anxious not to give a false impression of their lives. As Elizabeth Jane McCauley wrote from India: 'Do not think, my friends, that missionary work is easy or romantic; we often have to toil day in and day out with very little reward seemingly.'[70] Similarly, Miss Shaw regretted that there was 'so much routine, so little new or striking' that she found it difficult to 'tell her story in a new way' in the regular letters and reports expected by the home base.[71] Frequent furloughs from both the physical and emotional stresses of eastern life were seen as essential for rest and recuperation, although in fact these were usually spent in frantic rounds of speaking engagements designed to enhance funding and recruitment.[72]

During the years before the First World War the routine work of the mission was interrupted on several occasions by both natural and artificial crises. In 1889–90 famine in India, followed by an outbreak of cholera, filled orphanages to overflowing and resulted in extra effort both on the station and on the home front.[73] In China war with Japan in 1899–1900 was followed by the Boxer Rising of 1900, when anti-foreign feeling, sporadically expressed throughout the nineteenth century, erupted with concentrated ferocity. In this upsurge of violence 332 Chinese members of the Manchurian church were killed, together with forty-four Catholic and 130 Protestant missionaries and fifty of their children.[74] Although no members of the Irish Presbyterian mission were killed, they had to flee to Japan.[75] The diary of Dr Margaret McNeill graphically records the drama of this period, during which many mission buildings were lost and many Christian converts were martyred. Enclosed in her notebook are extracts from newspapers and reports detailing incidents of torture, abuse and death.[76] Far from discouraging missionary work, however, these events appear to have stimulated interest, generating an influx of both income and recruits. As Kathleen Bliss points out: 'though this falls under no category of Christian service, martyrdom has profoundly to do with the health and vitality of the Church and its power to propagate its faith'.[77]

Maintaining a steady supply of recruits was a constant problem for the Zenana Committee. The very success of the work, and the enthusiasm generated by workers at home and abroad, actually increased the demand for missionaries, while the nature of the work meant a fairly rapid turnover of personnel.[78] While a small number left the employ of the mission within one year, the average length of service between 1874 and 1914 was fifteen years, but there were wide variations within a range of two to forty years. Reasons for resignation varied, but the most common causes of early retirement were illness or marriage. Bill Addley notes that, of the sixty-four Zenana missionaries sent out between 1874 and 1910, thirteen retired because of ill health, while nine died in service.[79] Deaths were normally the result of disease, frequently exacerbated by weakness due to overwork.[80] Dr. Mary McGeorge, on the other hand, died when the ship on which she was returning from furlough was wrecked in 1893.[81]

Of the twenty-two Zenana missionaries who resigned before 1910 fifteen did so in order to marry other missionaries.[82] It seems that this type of work increased the likelihood of finding a partner from a similar background and with similar aspirations. Moreover, once married a new bride was clearly in a particularly strong position to continue her work by her husband's side, at least until the arrival of children limited her actions. While the Zenana Committee protected its investment by requiring the return of the costs of travel and salary of those who left its service within five years, such partnerships must have considerably strengthened the broader Christian mission.

How, then, do we measure or evaluate this aspect of 'women's work for women'? The Female Association was undoubtedly a successful business venture: a total of 124,983 pounds was collected between 1874 and 1911 (excluding interest and investments), and the value of estate and buildings in India and China amounted to a further 10,990 pounds. In mission stations in India and China five hospitals and two orphanages were fully staffed and operational, while two hospitals awaited workers and 2,700 pupils attended fifty-seven schools. Local workers trained by the mission comprised a doctor, twenty-four dispensers, 164 teachers and forty-two 'Biblewomen'.[83] These statistics attest to the sound financial and administrative management of local women, but, while it is relatively simple to acquire such statistical information, analysis of the mission's achievements is, of course, more complex. There is plenty of evidence, for example, that indigenous parents and children differed substantially from the missionary agents in their attitudes to education,[84] and that numerical counts of converts were unreliable. It is likely that missionary influence was more secular in nature than intended,[85] with both negative and positive consequences, and the role of Irishwomen needs to be put in the context of the wider relationship between Christian missions and imperial expansion, which dominated twentieth-century missionary historiography.

Although their lack of ordination ensured that in mainstream religious literature women in the mission field were long regarded as second-class citizens, Canadian, American and, more latterly, British writers have done much to address this imbalance. The purpose of this essay has been to initiate a similar re-evaluation of the work of Irish female Protestant missionaries; to enable us to begin to more accurately assess the implications, at home and abroad, of both the contribution they made and the rewards they reaped. Although the topic requires more extensive research, to enable us to fully comprehend the subtle shifts in status and power made possible by the missionary enterprise, it is already clear that for many young women in late nineteenth- and early twentieth-century Ireland, a combination of religious, cultural and educational influences, strength of personality, and lack of challenges on the home front made missionary work abroad an attractive option. As Rosemary Gagan has said of Canadian Methodist women missionaries: 'a professional female missionary body emerged which, in the context of limited career opportunities, enabled women to support themselves and to earn respect and authority as experts in mission affairs'.[86] The masses of women involved at the home base were given a new sphere of activism in which to operate, one that made a significant impact upon, and invigorated, their local meeting houses. Those holding office at the home base were given opportunities that, like those offered to their counterparts working abroad, enabled many of them 'to stay within the confines of socially sanctioned notions of femininity, yet stretch these boundaries and experience opportunities normally reserved for men'.[87] Perhaps most interesting is the supportive female atmosphere created by this dynamic network of women through close interaction between those working in the East and those praying, fundraising and recruiting at home. In both its practical and spiritual dimensions the work of the Female Association provides further evidence of the vast range of opportunities offered to women by the religious life in its varied forms.

CONVENT ARCHIVES AS SOURCES FOR IRISH HISTORY

Maria Luddy

The Women's History Project began its work in September 1997. It was initiated through the Women's History Association of Ireland and worked closely with the Irish Manuscripts Commission. The Project was set up to meet three main objectives: (a) to survey and record sources relevant to the history of women in Ireland; (b) to list these sources and to make the list available to the public through the provision of a CD-ROM; and (c) to publish historical documents relating to the history of women in Ireland.[1] Between October 1997 and June 1999 the Project undertook a survey of 420 public and private repositories in the Republic of Ireland and in Northern Ireland for collections or information relating to the history of women in Ireland from the earliest times to the present. *A Directory of Sources for Women's History in Ireland,* which contains information and descriptions of more than 14,000 collections and sources in 262 repositories, is the result of that survey. Among the archives and repositories visited were libraries, museums, diocesan archives, county council and corporation offices, and hospitals.

A prime source for the history of women in Ireland is, of course, convent archives. The records of a number of female religious congregations are also listed in the *Directory of Sources.* These records arguably contain the most extensive and underused collections of papers on Irish social and religious history from the late eighteenth century to the twentieth century.

Within the past ten years historians have begun to explore the importance of religious communities within Irish society.[2] The emphasis has moved away from finding heroines and models of piety among the nuns to analysing the general membership of religious communities; women's reasons for choosing a convent life; the various charitable, educational and welfare works of these communities; their internal structures; and nuns' relationships with each other, with church authorities and with the public generally. Recent discussion of convents and nuns has revolved around issues of autonomy and control, and the practical impact of female religious communities on the social and cultural development of Irish society since the late eighteenth century.

Before we examine some of the material available in convent archives, a short history of the development of convents in Ireland will provide some context for the valuable material to be found in these repositories.

CONVENT FOUNDATIONS

In 1800 there were six female religious orders in Ireland, with 120 nuns inhabiting eleven houses; by 1850 there were 1,500 nuns residing in ninety-five houses; and these numbers had risen to more than 8,000 living in 368 convents by 1901. These figures do not include the thousands of young women who were preparing to become nuns for the missions. For example, one convent school in County Kilkenny had up to 1,000 young women preparing to become missionaries in the 1870s.[3] As one historian has noted, much of the financial support for convents from the late eighteenth century onwards came from women, particularly women of the emerging wealthy middle classes.[4] A large number of the women who joined the communities in the early nineteenth century were from merchant families and they brought substantial sums of money to the convents they entered. For instance, Catherine Hayes, who entered the Presentation community in Carrick-on-Suir in January 1816, is stated to 'have brought a considerable property . . . and being highly educated she contributed largely to the advancement of the schools'.[5] It is clear from the records of convents that familial relationships were an important feature in their development. Sisters entered convents together; aunts and nieces joined, as well as cousins. In the published history of convents the impetus for establishing a community is usually given to a cleric. However, on looking through convent records, it is clear not only that many women provided the money for the foundation but that they were also anxious to institute a religious community.[6]

The support of clergymen was often vital for the survival of these early religious communities. Clergymen offered spiritual guidance, but they also offered practical support. Clerics, whether bishops or priests, could interfere as much or as little as they liked in convent affairs. For example, Dr Slattery, the bishop who had jurisdiction over the Thurles Presentation Convent, was adamant that the expenditure of the convent should not exceed its income. 'So particular was he', the convent annalist noted, 'that, with the exception of diet and clothing, he forbade the smallest outlay without his special leave.'[7]

CONVENT LOCATION

Although there were a few convents located in rural areas, most convents were established in urban communities. Nuns had to have financial support to ensure their continued existence. The dowries brought by sisters could offer some support. However, the capital sum could not be touched: this money had to be returned if a nun left, but the convents could use the interest earned from the capital. An urban setting allowed more individuals to donate funds to convents, and also allowed convents to provide a number of services that met the needs of the wider community.

Most convents were established in the richer provinces of Munster and Leinster. Again, this had much to do with the financial support available.[8] In the early years of foundations a typical dowry was in the region of 500 pounds, a considerable sum in early nineteenth-century Ireland. The requirement of a dowry remained an important part of women's ability to enter the religious life. Consider, for example, Anne M. Sargent, who was the daughter of a 'gentleman of wealth and position in Waterford'. Raised as a Protestant, Sargent was converted to Catholicism and met with a great deal of family opposition when she announced her intention to join the Presentation community in Waterford. Her father refused to provide the necessary dowry and Sargent's expenses were met initially by Edmund Rice, the founder of the Christian Brothers. In 1810 she went as a postulant to the convent in Cork. By this time her father had agreed to pay 500 pounds as a dowry, but the money was not ready when the time came for Sargent's profession. Sargent then completed a third noviciate in Clonmel and was finally professed in 1816, after her father relented. Sargent was later elected superior of the convent and it was she, as Sister M. Magdalen, who led a new foundation to Manchester in 1835. Sargent, who played a major role in the development of the

Clonmel community, was obviously a serious and determined candidate for the religious life, yet without a dowry it took her nine years to be professed.[9] However, as the nineteenth century progressed smaller sums, allied to training or other skills, served the function of the earlier larger dowries.[10]

Women who entered convents generally joined in their mid-twenties. However, when convents were being established in the late eighteenth and early nineteenth centuries older women also joined these communities. The number of entrants increased as the nineteenth century progressed. The expansion of religious congregations made their work more widely known and among their attractions they offered young women active roles in society.

THE FOUNDERS OF IRISH CONVENTS

The founders of the native Irish convents were generally women of independent wealth. Among these women were Nano Nagle, who was instrumental in establishing the Presentation Order, finally approved by Rome in 1809; Mary Aikenhead, who formed the Sisters of Charity in 1815; Catherine McAuley, founder of the Sisters of Mercy in 1831; and Margaret Aylward, founder of the Sisters of the Holy Faith in 1867.

Nano Nagle had been educated in France and had passed an unsuccessful noviciate in a convent there. She began to organise poor schools in Cork City, at a time when the Penal Laws were still on the statute books. In the late 1760s her schools were threatened with closure unless they could be provided with some form of permanence. For this reason Nagle asked the Ursulines, a French order, to take over the schools, which they did in 1771. Nagle herself did not join the Ursuline convent and was unhappy with the way that the schools were conducted. The Ursulines were an enclosed order and therefore could not leave the convent to teach in other schools that Nagle had established. In order to continue her work with the poor, Nagle, with three other women, established the Sisters of Charitable Instruction in Cork in 1775. She was also in touch with a lay woman, Teresa Mulally (1728–1803), who was educating the poor in Dublin around the same time as Nagle was conducting her poor schools in Cork. Mulally had organised a group of lay women who took religious vows. This group joined with Nagle's Sisters of Charitable Instruction in 1794 and became the Presentation Order.[11]

Catherine McAuley, founder of the Sisters of Mercy, is a particularly interesting woman of this period. McAuley was born in Dublin on 29 September 1778 and, although baptised a Catholic, was raised as a Protestant. It was from her Protestant guardian that she inherited a large fortune in 1824. She had already engaged in charitable work around the city of Dublin and now used her inheritance to establish a hostel for homeless women in Baggot Street. This 'House of Mercy' was opened in September 1827. McAuley gathered a group of women around her who were also interested in her philanthropic work and they lived together as a community, taking informal religious vows and being free to return to their own homes whenever they wished. McAuley attempted to extend the work of her House of Mercy in 1829 and publicly solicited funds for her project. It was from this time that concerted opposition to this community of laywomen became evident, much of it coming from the Catholic clergy, with the priests in her own parish showing particular hostility towards the group. McAuley's Protestant background and the fact that she was not a member of the Catholic gentry made her vulnerable to clerical opposition.[12] There were concerns that her project would rival and divert funds away from Mary Aikenhead's Sisters of Charity, established in 1815, while Archbishop Murray and many other clerics disapproved of an organisation that had some of the characteristics of a religious community but was in fact made up of laywomen, and over which they had no control. Discussions with the archbishop left McAuley with a choice: to remove the religious appearance of her community, or to organise it along strictly religious lines and come under the jurisdiction of the clergy. It took McAuley six months to decide to form a religious community.[13] Towards the end of her life she wrote: 'I never intended founding a religious congregation, all I wanted was to serve the poor since that seemed to be what God expected of me.'[14] This remark can be seen as a token of humility, a trait constantly alluded to in the biographies of nuns; or we can read it as a revelation of the very real difficulties that McAuley experienced in attempting to manage her philanthropic work and her congregation after its foundation. McAuley, in fact, established what is now the second largest religious congregation of women in the world.

In the early nineteenth century entering a convent was a means for women to assert their independence. As the century progressed, however, that independence came under the direction of the reorganised church and convents became more institutionalised. By the end of the century bishops often visited convents and clerical interference with the internal affairs of a community became much more common. Ultimate authority in convent life lay with clerics. Nuns who were unhappy with community life often appealed to clerics to make changes within the convent or to allow them to leave the community. On occasion priests forced convents to hand over their financial affairs to them, often with disastrous consequences. However, many convent superiors were adept at advancing the interests of their communities. The use of language that tends to equate nuns with humility and submissiveness in their dealings with clerics masks the level of manipulation and real power that convent superiors were able to exert. For instance, Frances Ball, founder of the Loreto Order, wrote to one of the sisters of the order in 1862 that, in dealings with bishops, 'minute transactions should not be communicated to the Bishop, if the Superioress can arrange them, but matters of consequence should not be undertaken without his Lordship's advice and approbation'.[15] In this same letter Ball also made clear the limits of the bishop's power in the internal affairs of the convent: 'The Bishop has not the appointment of local superiors. If the Bishop order any measure compatible with our holy rules, all must submit, if the measure be found inconvenient, the Bishop may respectfully be informed of the general opinion, for an alteration of the order.' The Sisters of Charity, for instance, had some difficulty with Bishop Murphy in the early days of their foundation in Cork. Mary Aikenhead, in her letters to the convent superior, reveals both her political acumen and her diplomatic skills. Her letter to Mary de Chantal Coleman notes:

> In regard to your anxiety about attending the new schools, do not allow that to rest a moment on your mind . . . Unless the bishop be much changed, I have good reason to know that our attempting anything of the kind would displease him . . . Our line of duty is straightforward and, except to express the fact that it belongs to our vocation to undertake such works as may be proposed (if it does so), we should refrain from expressing

anxiety to be so employed, and you can always say that 'the bishop knows all we may be employed in, if it be his pleasure so to employ us'.[16]

INTERNAL CONVENT POLITICS

It is evident that female religious communities did not challenge class relationships and that a two-tier system class division operated within convents themselves. In all the histories of convents written by nuns or clerics throughout the nineteenth and twentieth centuries almost no reference is made to lay sisters. Lay nuns are the least visible members of religious communities. The internal hierarchical structure of the convent rested on the distinction between lay nuns and choir nuns. Lay sisters were generally from humble backgrounds and carried out the domestic tasks of the communities. Essentially they were the domestic servants of the communities, in a society that had very clear notions about the place of servants. Choir nuns were from wealthier backgrounds, were well-educated and carried out the public work for which the communities had been established. Choir nuns never engaged in domestic tasks, while lay nuns rarely made any public contribution to the work of a religious community. Lay entrants to a community were always fewer than choir entrants.

The division between lay and choir nuns was not just a customary or traditional one, but was consciously institutionalised in the rules and regulations of the community. In the *Mercy Guide Book*, for example, the lives of lay and choir nuns were considered distinct. Recreation and meals were always taken separately. They were also distinguished by their terms of address. Lay nuns had to prefix the names of choir sisters with the terms 'Mrs' and those of choir novices with 'Miss'; lay nuns were all called 'Sister'. The most distinguishing feature was, of course, their dress. The habits for both the lay and choir nuns were described in great detail, and that of a lay nun very much resembled the domestic attire of Victorian female servants. Lay nuns were required to be subservient to choir nuns, and such subservience was evidenced in the language, rituals and symbolism of convent life.[17]

Strict class divisions, as reflected in the existence of lay and choir nuns, were intended to create an harmonious working unit. However, ethnic tensions also sometimes appeared and could be divisive within communities. For example, in the establishment of the Bermondsey Mercy Convent in London Catherine McAuley had placed Mother Clare, a nun from Cork, in charge of the new community. This created friction between Mother Clare and the English sisters, who did not wish to have an Irish woman as their superior. McAuley was to learn from that experience and when she went on to make a foundation in Birmingham she appointed an English woman, Juliana Hardman, as superior. McAuley was to write: 'I think [that] Birmingham will be a most flourishing house, and Bermondsey is all alive since Paddy [Mother M. Clare] left . . . amongst the most amiable we could clearly discover a desire that "John Bull" be the head on all occasions.'[18] Ethnic tensions existed in foundations made in Africa, Asia and the Americas, with the Irish sisters often seeing themselves as superior to the indigenous populations.[19]

The religious life could be liberating for many women. Once within the convent some women found opportunities for advancement and self-expression, achieving positions of authority and power that were unavailable to lay women. The most important and influential positions within the convent were those of Reverend Mother, Mother Assistant, Bursar and Mistress of Novices. Often, and particularly in the early years of a community's existence, the same women held these posts over different periods. While there were definite guidelines about the length of time positions of authority could be held by any person within a community, these were often ignored. In the Presentation Order, for example, a superior was to be elected every three years, had to be at least thirty years of age and had to have been professed for at least five years. However, a superior who proved to be exceptional could often hold onto this important post for a number of years. In Cashel, for instance, Lucy Ryan was elected superior in 1857, a post she held until her death in 1877.[20]

The Reverend Mother held the primary position of power within the convent. She was helped by the Mother Assistant, who deputised in her absence. The Bursar worked closely with the Reverend Mother, controlling the finances of the community. The Novice Mistress directed the noviciate. She had considerable influence in determining which novices completed their training, and also identified women who would later be given positions of power and authority in the community. The position of Reverend Mother was determined by election amongst the choir nuns; she in turn nominated sisters for the other positions and these were then accepted or rejected by the Chapter. Lay sisters played no part in the process of election or in the process of decision-making that governed community life. Although we are often told that women who join or joined religious communities did so out of a sense of vocation, this rhetoric should not blind us to the practical advantages women might have expected of convent life.

CONVENT ARCHIVES

The richness of convent archives for a study of Irish history has not yet been fully recognised by historians. Research in such archives is not solely a means of examining the lives of nuns, and exploring the internal physical, spiritual and emotional spaces where these women lived out their lives. Through convent archives we can also study the history of Irish society generally, using a wide variety of techniques and disciplines.

The architecture of convents and their attached institutions reveals the use of space, internal and external, where nuns carried out their lives and managed their charges. Convents, particularly those that had institutions attached, were apparent public buildings, clearly evident on the geographical landscape, but the physical space of these buildings was carefully defined and regulated. For instance, within a convent the parlour and the chapel marked the boundaries of public access to the interior. The place of convents within the physical landscape of Irish towns is significant in terms of mapping the extent of institutional presence in the country. The extensive nature of foreign missionary activity can also be mapped from convent records. It is interesting to note that the construction of convents or extensions to their buildings was often overseen, in even the smallest detail, by the superior of the community.

Through convent archives we can also uncover the history of health, welfare, and educational institutions of all types in Ireland. We can, to some extent, examine the lives of individuals who came into contact with religious communities, whether as children or adults, as users of services, as providers of money and funding, as representatives of higher authorities. The material stored in convent archives holds the history not only of religious congregations but also of Irish society itself.

The quality and quantity of the material held in the various archives varies to a great extent. Many records have been lost over the years: correspondence can be destroyed, and registers and other large volumes may be cleared out to make room for newer material. Natural disasters such as fires have also depleted the records of some communities. While convent archivists and sisters themselves are now very aware of the historical importance of their work, nuns, like their lay counterparts in business or welfare work, have found in the past that the day-to-day business of living and working has not always made record preservation a priority.

Generally, convent archives can be divided into community records and institutional records.[21] Records of the community include the annals, in which are written the significant events of the community's history. Convent annals form the 'official' history of the community. In some cases 'good' annals have been transcribed, and sometimes edited, from earlier written annals. Sometimes pages have been cut out of annals. For instance, Sr M. Dominic Kelly notes in her history of the Sligo Ursulines that in one set of manuscripts twenty pages are missing from 1835. She contends that the pages were cut because they gave an unfavourable account of the reasons why a sister had left the community in Ennis. Similarly, it is noted that another set of annals was written up at the request of a Reverend Mother and that the author was directed to be 'uncontroversial'.[22] Annals were often written retrospectively by a member of the community. They record the major events in the community's life, the deaths of sisters, the work of the community, and its relationship with clerics and the public in general. Annals are the history of the community and are not written for a public audience.

Sometimes extracts from convent annals are published in various congregational histories. One of the more interesting publications in this regard is the *Leaves from the Annals of the Sisters of Mercy*, first produced in 1884, which crosses the divide between the private world of the convent and the public world of the lay Catholic. The *Annals*, written by Mother Austin Mary Carroll, was clearly written for public consumption and provides an excellent overview of the development of the Mercy congregation in the nineteenth century.[23] Carroll had a definite purpose in publishing a history of the community: she wished to make the life and work of Catherine McAuley more widely known to the public. The *Annals* was very much welcomed by Mercy congregations around the world, but some communities found the author 'too frank about adverse circumstances'.[24] In her chronicle Carroll is much more revealing of the difficulties faced by the congregation than contemporary chroniclers of other religious communities. This volume still provides the fullest account of the spread of the congregation throughout Ireland.

Also to be found within convent archives are copies of constitutions. The constitutions detail the rights and responsibilities of each office, and outline the expected behaviour of the sisters in the community, their duties towards each other and towards the congregation. In many instances constitutions were constructed with the assistance of clerics, but in some cases they were written by founding sisters. Indeed, the evidence of the constitutions reveals the intellectual abilities of convent founders.

Allied to the constitutions, and of vital importance in understanding the intellectual and spiritual development of religious communities, are their libraries. In some communities lists of books have been kept, although unfortunately, with the closure of many larger convent buildings, some of the libraries have been dispersed.

Convents almost always have a register of women who have entered the community. These registers record the name, parents' names, and dates of entry, noviciateship and profession of each woman. From such registers statistics can be gathered about the social status of entrants, their age and other data. In addition to this information many communities have records relating to the dowries women brought to the convent with them. As we have noted, a number of sisters brought substantial fortunes to the convent.

The financial records of many communities also survive, often revealing the names of those who provided donations to the convent or subscribed to its enterprises. Many of the financial records also account for the day-to-day spending of the community and the costs of running attached institutions. Thus one can track the prices of foodstuffs and clothing over a number of years, as well as the cost of services such as building repairs, gardening and other matters. Convent superiors had, in many cases, to supply yearly data on their income and expenditure to the local bishop. Convents were, in many instances, managed as business enterprises, with the difference that all profits went back into the wider community through investment in the convents's own work. A number of convents were substantial landowners, and records exist of disputes between tenants and their convent 'landlords'. Convents also invested money in stocks and shares, and again records of these investments exist in many communities.

Of great interest to historians is the correspondence that survives within these archives. This details links with families, clerics and other authorities. Much of the correspondence from superiors, particularly founders, offers spiritual and practical advice to sisters in branch convents. The correspondence within these archives can be complemented by that available in various diocesan archives. Letters in these repositories provide insights into relationships between nuns and bishops and priests in general.

In some instances diaries of sisters are also to be found in the convent archives. While some of the diaries record information of a personal nature, there are a number describing the work engaged in by the sisters. For instance, the diary of Mother Catherine of the Sisters of Charity, which runs from 2 July 1812 to 29 August 1825, details visitations to the poor and gives descriptions of their living conditions. Similarly, many of the fifteen nuns from Ireland who arrived in the Crimea in December 1854, to nurse the sick and wounded British soldiers who were fighting in the Crimean War, kept journals of their experiences. Only three of these journals appear to have survived. They recorded the conditions under which the nuns travelled to the Crimea, the state of the hospitals they worked in, their relationships with the soldiers, and with medical and military authorities, and their troubled relationship with Florence Nightingale. Relations between Nightingale and the Irish Sisters began badly and deteriorated as the war continued. The leader of the Irish group, Mother Francis Bridgeman, in her first negotiations with Nightingale noted that she had 'an ambitious woman to deal with on whom she could not rely'. These journals provide a unique insight into the power relations that existed between the nuns and Nightingale, and a fresh perspective on Nightingale's role in the administration of hospitals in the East.[25]

Institutional records form a major portion of convent archives. Most often these records consist of registers of the inmates of various institutional establishments. Nuns have managed industrial and reformatory schools, and magdalen asylums; they have founded hospitals and nursed in workhouse infirmaries.[26] For example, during the late eighteenth century and throughout the nineteenth century there were about thirty-five magdalen asylums in Ireland. Most were based in Dublin, but there were also homes in such places as Limerick, Galway, Cork, Belfast, Derry, Waterford and Tralee. Catholic nuns, particularly the Sisters of the Good Shepherd, the Sisters of Mercy and the Sisters of Charity, ran the majority of these refuges. The registers of these asylums provide details of the inmates, such as their names, their former places of residence and how they came to the institution.[27]

Much of the work of nuns revolved around education. School roll books, together with details of boarding schools, the curriculum followed and reports of the inspection of schoolwork, are also available.

Records of associations such as the Children of Mary, confraternities, sodalities and pioneer total abstinence societies can also be found in some convent archives. Some of the work of nuns also involved sick visitation, and records were kept of the numbers of sick persons visited, as well as registers of visits made to prisons. In some cases the financial records of these various associations and institutions have also been preserved. Visual material is also available in some archives, and this includes maps and plans of buildings, photographs, diaries, films, tapes, and press cuttings. Legal documents such as wills and indentures are also to be found.

The range of material outlined above provides some idea of the extensive nature of convent records. While the concentration has been on the history of communities, it should not be forgotten that the records available relate to issues of welfare and the social, economic and religious history of Ireland. A few examples of the broader implications of the material available will provide some indication of how valuable the sources are for Irish history generally.

For instance, the Medical Missionaries of Mary have a substantial archive of material. Mother Mary Martin founded the Medical Missionaries in April 1937.[28] Their archive contains about 150 boxes of material. This is made up of correspondence, diaries, minute books, press cuttings, photographs, films and some tapes. Many of the documents are letters between members of the congregation and the Superior General. There is much detail concerning the foundation of the congregation, and the staffing of new foundations in Ireland, the United States, Italy, several African countries and other countries as far away as Taiwan and Brazil. Among the treasures of this collection are the papers of Marie Martin from 1892. These include correspondence with her mother between 1915 and 1921, when Martin worked as a Voluntary Aid Detachment (VAD) nurse in Malta and France. The history of Irish women in the First World War still needs to be written and the papers of Marie Martin will be an invaluable aid to that history. Recent work on women at the front has raised questions about the power dynamics that existed between soldiers and nurses, and between different groups of women workers at the front, whether as VADs, army nurses or relief workers.[29] The war and nursing experiences revealed in Marie Martin's letters support many of the findings of historians of this subject. In January 1916, for instance, Martin wrote to her mother about various regulations intended to keep nurses from socialising with their patients, which meant that she and the matron, when accompanying the men on a Christmas treat, had to travel in a separate railway carriage and pretend that they had encountered the soldiers by chance.[30] Martin also mentions the rivalry between VADs and army nurses, which was a feature of women's war experiences at the Front: in a tea shop she observed some VADs, contrary to regulations, chatting to officers from the hospital ship. She and her friends left, 'leaving the other little fools talking and laughing and the two Army sisters taking it all in'.[31]

The archive of the Medical Missionaries of Mary also holds the records of the Waterford Maternity Hospital, which was established as the Waterford Lying-In Hospital in about 1838, although records exist from 1834. The hospital functioned under the management of a group of twelve ladies known as the Waterford Maternity Hospital Committee and was funded by charitable donations. There are fifteen bound volumes recording the day-to-day workings of the hospital between 1833 and 1969. These include a volume listing deliveries between 1833 and 1839; a Matron's Book, which includes details on patients, linen supplies and so on between 1840 and 1849; a register that records the numbers of births between 1855 and 1906; and a register of patients between 1883 and 1912. Also in this collection are two volumes of minutes of the committee, between January 1882 and January 1893, and between February 1894 and October 1904, together with three volumes of account books from 1862 to 1930.

Indeed, many convent archives have substantial material relating to the history of medicine in Ireland. In 1834 the Sisters of Charity established St Vincent's Hospital in Dublin. Before the opening of that hospital Mary Aikenhead, founder of the community, had sent three of the sisters of her order to the Hospital of Notre Dame de la Pitié in Paris to be trained by the Sisters of St Thomas of Villanova.[32] St Vincent's was the first hospital in Dublin to provide care specifically for the Catholic population. The Sisters of Mercy followed the Sisters of Charity into hospital work when they opened the Mercy Hospital in Cork city in 1857 and the Mater Hospital in Dublin in 1861. Other hospitals were opened in Belfast and Limerick in the last decades of the nineteenth century.[33]

Nuns also played important roles in workhouse hospitals. In 1861 the Limerick Board of Guardians was the first to win permission from the Poor Law Commissioners to allow nuns to nurse in their workhouse hospital. Workhouse hospitals, particularly from the 1850s, became increasingly important centres of public health care, a fact recognised by the Poor Law Commissioners as early as 1854.[34] By 1895 sixty-three boards of guardians had placed their workhouse infirmaries in the care of nuns; by 1903 that number had increased to eighty-four and just over half of the workhouse hospitals were staffed by nuns, most often the Sisters of Mercy, although the Sisters of St John of God and the Sisters of Charity of St Vincent de Paul also nursed in these hospitals.[35] In 1884 the Ennis Board of Guardians spent some time discussing the possibility of employing two nuns and paying each of them twenty or thirty pounds a year. Eventually it was pointed out that if two nuns were appointed more would come with them to form the community.[36] Accepting a low salary was, in a number of instances at least, a strategy used by the nuns to make them more acceptable to boards of guardians. For instance, Mother M. Joseph Perry of the Ennis community asked advice from the Mercy Sisters in Limerick about securing access to the workhouse infirmaries. She was informed that:

> In order not to increase the prejudices of those hostile to the movement Rev. Mother Moore [Reverend Mother in Limerick in 1861] avoided raising difficulties about things not absolutely important, especially about money matters, a point on which fears were entertained by opponents. We could not get into the hospital at all except as paid nurses. So she named the low salary of 20 pounds per annum, refused to take the rations that would have been given, but accepted coal and light. Since [then] we have found that it would have been a great convenience to have taken milk.[37]

Nuns who had such experience of home and hospital nursing were, in fact, medical practitioners in their own right. The nuns performed a range of medical functions within the workhouse infirmaries. They managed the diet of the sick, clearly an important therapeutic tool. They also performed minor surgical procedures, such as dressing wounds, lancing boils, administering medicines and stimulants, and so on.[38] The *Guide for the Religious Called Sisters of Mercy*, a book of more than 400 pages covering Mercy Sisters' work in the public domain and their conduct within the private arena of the convent, stressed that nurses should be able to meet sudden medical emergencies when medical aid might not be at hand: they might, for example, be called on to stop bleeding after an operation.

To gain the clearest picture of the place of nuns in workhouses it is necessary to consult diocesan archives. In this regard the Elphin Diocesan Archives contain a number of files on the state of nursing in Irish workhouses. Information was gathered about the conditions in workhouse hospitals with the purpose making a case for the admission of nuns as nurses. A letter dated 14 February 1898 from the Local Government Board to Sligo Union on the inspection of the workhouse noted that:

> Dr Flynn points out that the arrangement[s] for nursing in the Union hospitals are far from satisfactory. It appears that the present staff consists of three principal nurses one of whom holds a certificate in training in midwifery; the other two have had some hospital experience but do not hold certificates. There are also two night nurses, one for the upper hospital (female) and the other for the male hospital. In addition there are two night attendants for the idiot wards. All of these it appears are untrained, and up to some time ago were paupers but now receive a small salary and rations. The nursing staff is augmented by a large number of pauper wardsmen and one or two wardswomen – seventeen or eighteen in all who assist in the nursing.[39]

Among the oldest convent records are those held by the Dominican Order. Dominican women in Galway were recognised and approved as a community of nuns by the Irish Provincial Chapter that met in Kilkenny in 1643. The exiled Sister Julian Nolan and Sister Mary Lynch returned to Galway in 1686. Eight sisters arrived in Dublin from Galway in the spring of 1717 and moved to Channel Row after residing for six months in Fisher Lane. The bulk of the collection in the Dominican archives in Dublin dates from the 1920s,[40] but there is some older material from the eighteenth century that relates to the Channel Row convent. This includes account and receipt books from 1719; there are also inventories, lists of debts, bonds and lists of lodgers. There is also material about the instruction of novices, community life and the educational work of the Order. For the nineteenth and twentieth centuries, for instance, account books for the Immaculata boarding school are available from 1835; there are also report books from the period 1889–1973, and lists of exam results and student prizegivings from the years 1835–1921.

Records of other communities also throw light on the education provided in many of the convent boarding schools of the period. In the Loreto archives we find letters of that order's founder, Frances Ball, relating to the nature of the education provided to the pupils. Writing from Rathfarnham in Dublin in November 1851 Ball notes:

> We have 10 novices, 3 postulants, 64 boarders, 16 day pupils, 125 poor children here. All are enjoying health and prosperity . . . The last Saturday of every month, each boarder plays a separate piece of music, the others repair their garments. 70 learn the *piano forte*. We have a music teacher from Dublin, 6 days in the week: one nun has 20 music pupils. The first Tuesday of the month, the Mistress of Schools reads aloud the judgements of the pupils written by their instructresses; on these reports the premiums from France are annually distributed . . . Books of history and of geography are read aloud in the Young Ladies' Refectory, of which they write an account. They are questioned on portions of these historical works, on 1st Tuesday. The explanation of the Christian Doctrine falls daily to me, our pupils write a résumé of these instructions, all their exercise books are shown on each first Tuesday of the month, and their pieces of music, for which each one has a portfolio.[41]

When the Sisters of Mercy arrived in Kilrush, County Clare, they took charge of a local school that had 588 girls enrolled as pupils, although school attendance rarely rose above 300. This school was affiliated to the National Board and when a new building was erected a cross had been placed on the gable wall. Schools under the National Board were to be non-denominational and the school inspector requested that the cross be removed. The annals noted:

> The inspector expressed himself entirely satisfied with the standard of education imparted but directed that the cross be removed. A vigorous correspondence ensued between the board and the pastor, the former requiring that the cross should be taken down, the latter positively refusing to remove it. The priest triumphed for the present. A year or two later the crusade was again renewed by the National School Board and for a year they refused payment to the monitresses because the cross held its place. But sooner than remove the cross the Sisters were willing to sever their connection from the Board as others had done. Finally its officers wisely thought proper to say no more on the subject.[42]

Indeed, it would be impossible to investigate the history of the education of women and girls in Ireland without examining the records of convent-run national, pension and secondary schools.

The range of material available in convent archives has only been touched on here, but I hope that even this brief review will alert researchers to their potential value. It must, however, be remembered that convent archives are private records. Not all convents have the resources or facilities to assist researchers. It can sometimes be very difficult to gain access to records, particularly those relating to the twentieth century. Records of reformatories and industrial schools are currently closed to researchers, as are records of magdalen asylums. However, approaches can be made to community archivists in respect of research that involves other areas of their work, such as education. Generally, approaches to research the history of a community and their work are looked on favourably, provided that the community has facilities to allow the research. Requests to undertake research should be made in writing in the first instance to the archivist of the community. The *Directory of Sources for Women's History in Ireland* provides further detail on convent collections and information on how to gain access to these sources.

J'AI MAL À NOS DENTS

Eiléan Ní Chuilleanáin

I wrote this poem not long after the death of my father's youngest sister, Anna. She had joined a religious order called the Franciscans of Calais in her twenties. None of my three aunts who entered convents did so straight from school; perhaps this relates to the fact that they were of a somewhat lower social class than many nuns, although reasonably well-educated.

In a railwayman's family of seven my father was the only boy. He was the only one whose education was important, the only one to go to college, the only one to marry and the first to die. Life at home was rigidly religious – and I use the word 'rigid' advisedly – but he was exempted from attendance at family prayers because of his need to study. For the girls there was no way out except the way of the convent – my grandmother was determined that none of them should marry. It has always seemed to me, knowing my aunts, that the three sisters who became nuns did so to escape, in the only way they could, from their mother's strictness, into a way of life that was certainly rigid enough in the early days, but also offered them both spiritual and worldly adventures.

Anna went to Calais to the novitiate and there learned French, which she always spoke well and forcefully, and assimilated the ways of the convent. These included acquiring new 'mothers' and 'sisters', and the habit of never saying 'mine' about anything. In my childhood nuns said 'our shoe', 'our stocking'. When Anna went to the dentist she said 'I have a pain in our teeth' and he thought she was mad.

My poem, then, is partly a celebration of her life and adventures as she told them to me as a teenager and later, usually in a mixture of French and English. She returned to Ireland in her fifties but liked to speak French to me; it represented a part of her life and her mind that she did not want to lose. After she died I wrote the French phrases into the poem, partly because they were typical of her, partly because as an Irish poet I have always wanted to write a macaronic poem and partly because I did not want my surviving aunts in Cork to understand

116

too much. The phrases are earthy and clear-sighted, like Anna: 'I was half-pissed'; 'I'll be eating dandelions by the roots' – i.e. 'I'll be dead'; 'One sick person to look after another'. I also intended the poem as a tribute to other women of her kind. I have read the poem to diverse audiences and had responses from people who knew women like Anna, whether Irish-American pioneering nuns or German Protestant deaconesses who worked in the chaos of war and displacement of peoples.

The other side of the poem is that it is a meditation on language, and the way it designates the family and the body of the speaker. It was first published in a collection called *Confounded Language* with images by the artist Noel Connor. When I was asked for a poem for that collection I thought of my aunt with her two families and her two languages, and the international dimension of her life at a time when we think of Irish women's lives as confined and inward-looking. The connection with Catholic Europe was, as Kate O'Brien's fiction shows, a way for women to discover themselves through new languages and strange places.

J'AI MAL À NOS DENTS

In memory of Anna Cullinane (Sister Mary Antony)

The Holy Father gave her leave
To return to her father's house
At seventy-eight years of age.

When young in the Franciscan house at Calais
She complained to the dentist, *I have a pain in our teeth*
– Her body dissolving out of her first mother,
– Her five sisters aching at home.

Her brother listened to news
Five times in a morning on Radio Eireann
In Cork, as the Germans entered Calais.
Her name lay under the surface, he could not see her
Working all day with the sisters,
Stripping the hospital, loading the sick on lorries,

While Reverend Mother walked the wards and nourished them
With jugs of wine to hold their strength.
J'étais à moitié saoule. It was done,
They lifted the old sisters on to the pig-car
And the young walked out on the road to Desvres,
The wine still buzzing and the planes over their heads.

Je mangerai les pissenlits par les racines.
A year before she died she lost her French accent
Going home in her habit to care for her sister Nora
(*Une malade à soigner une malade*).
They handed her back her body,
Its voices and its death.

NOTES

NOTES TO INTRODUTION

1. For a sample of St Paul's views on women see Galatians, Ch. 3, 28, Ephesians, Ch. 5, 22–24 and 1 Timothy, Ch. 2, 11–12.
2. On these developments, see K. Thomas, 'Women and the Civil War sects', *Past and Present*, no. 13, April 1958, pp. 42–62; Phil Kilroy, 'Women and the Reformation in Seventeenth-century Ireland', Margaret MacCurtain and Mary O'Dowd eds, *Women in early modern Ireland*, (1991) pp. 179–196; Ruth Liebowitz, 'Virgins in the service of Christ: the dispute over an active apostolate for women during the Counter-Reformation', Eleanor McLaughlin and Rosemary Ruether eds, *Women of spirit*, (1979) pp. 132–51.
3. Sarah Lewis, *Woman's mission* (1839) quoted in Jane Rendall, *The origins of modern feminism: women in Britain, France and the United States, 1780–1860*, (1985) p. 75.
4. Margaret MacCurtain, 'Religion, science, theology and ethics, 1500–2000', *The Field Day Anthology of Irish Writing*, vol. IV, (2002) pp. 459–63, p. 459.
5. Margaret MacCurtain and Donncha O'Corrain eds, *Women in Irish society: the historical dimension*, (1978).
6. Caitriona Clear, *Nuns in nineteenth-century Ireland*, (1987).
7. See, for example, Suellen Hoy and Margaret MacCurtain, *From Dublin to New Orleans: The Journey of Nora and Alice*, (1994); Jacinta Prunty, *Margaret Aylward, 1810–1889*, (1995); Mary Peckham Magray, *The Transforming Power of the Nuns: Women, Religion and Cultural Change in Ireland, 1750–1900*, (1998); Maria Luddy ed., *The Crimean Journals of the Sisters of Mercy*, (2004); David Hempton and Myrtle Hill, *Evangelical Protestantism in Ulster Society, 1740–1890*, (1992); Janice Holmes, *Religious Revivals in Britain and Ireland, 1859–1905*, (2000); Maria Luddy, *Women and Philanthropy in Nineteenth-Century Ireland*, (1995). See also essays on female spirituality and faith-inspired action in collections such as Mary Cullen (ed), *Girls Don't Do Honours: Irishwomen in Education in the Nineteenth and Twentieth Centuries*, (1987); Maria Luddy and Cliona Murphy (eds), *Women Surviving: Studies in Irish Women's History in the Nineteenth and Twentieth Centuries*, (1989); Margaret MacCurtain and Mary O'Dowd (eds), *Women in Early Modern Ireland*, (1991); Janice Holmes and Diane Urquhart (eds), *Coming Into the Light: The Work, Politics and Religion of Women in Ulster, 1840–1940*, (1994); Maryann Gialanella Valiulis and Mary O'Dowd (eds), *Women and Irish History*, (1997); Mary Cullen and Maria Luddy (eds), *Women, Power and Consciousness in Nineteenth-Century Ireland*, (1995); Alan Hayes and Diane Urquhart (eds), *Irish Women's History*, (2004).

NOTES TO PHIL KILROY

1. Madeleine Sophie Barat (1779–1865) was born in Joigny, France into a lower bourgeois family. She received most of her formal education from her brother, Louis, first in Joigny and later in Paris. In 1800, she joined a religious association of women called the Dilette di Gesu, involved in female education in Amiens. This association was dissolved in 1804. By 1815 Sophie Barat and her companions had established a new community called the Society of the Sacred Heart, which expanded throughout and beyond France. By the time of Sophie Barat's death, in 1865, the Society of the Sacred Heart had eighty-nine houses together with boarding and poor schools in Europe, North and South America, and Africa. Madeleine Sophie Barat was canonised by the Catholic Church in 1925.

2. Virginia Woolf, *Orlando* (London, 1992), p. 202.

3. Carolyn G. Heilbrun, *Writing a Woman's Life* (London, 1989), p. 51.

4. Adéle Cahier, *Vie de la Venerable Mére Madeleine Sophie Barat, Fondatrice et Première Supérieure Générale de la Société du Sacré Cœur*, 2 vols (Paris, 1884); Louis Baunard, *Histoire de Madame Barat, Fondatrice de la Société du Sacré Cœur*, 2 vols (Paris, 1876).

5. Phil Kilroy, *Madeleine Sophie Barat: a Life* (Cork, 2000). Also published in French and Spanish.

6. Gérard Cholvy, *Être chrétien en France au XIXe siècle, 1790–1914* (Paris, 1997), pp. 11–19, 143; Ralph Gibson, *A Social History of French Catholicism* (London,1989), pp. 14–29.

7. Geneviève Gadbois, '"Vous êtes presque la seule consolation de l'Église": la foi des femmes face à la déchristianisation de 1789–1880' in Jean Delumeau (ed.), *La religion de ma mère. Le rôle des femmes dans la transmission de la foi* (Paris, 1992), pp. 301–25.

8. Claude Langlois, *Le catholicisme au féminin. Les congrégations françaises à supérieure générale au XIXe siècle* (Paris, 1984); Odile Arnold, *Le corps et l'âme. La vie religieuse au XIXe siècle* (Paris, 1984); Yvonne Turin, *Femmes et religieuses au XIXe siècle* (Paris, 1989); Denis Peletier, *Les catholiques en France depuis 1815* (Paris, 1997), pp. 28–30; Cholvy, *Être chrétien en France*, pp. 36–45; Ralph Gibson, 'Le catholicisme et les femmes en France au XIXe siècle' in *Revue d'histoire de l'église de France*, vol. lxxix, no. 202 (janvier–juin, 1993), pp. 63–93; Elizabeth and Robert Rapley, 'The Image of Religious Women in the *Ancien Régime: The États des Religieuses of 1790–1791*' in *French History*, vol. 11, no. 4, (Dec. 1997), pp. 387–410.

9. On this topic, see Alison Weber, *Teresa of Avila and the Rhetoric of Femininity* (Princeton, 1990).

10. Edme Davier, *Miscellanea eruditionis tam sacrae quam profanae*, in S. Jossier, 'Notice sur Edme-Louis Davier' in *Bulletin de la Société des Sciences de l'Yonne [BSSY]*, vol. 13 (1859), p. 144; 'Quelques personnages illustres: Edme-Louis Davier (1665–1746)' in *Notre Saint-Thibault. Bulletin Paroissial*, 1e novembre 1937, no. 4. Original text: *Une femme . . . est un[e] protégé[e] qui change de figure et de caractère comme il lui plaît. Dissimulée dans ses pensées, ingénieuses dans ses passions, politiques dans ses vues, friponne dans ses discours, coquette dans ses manières, affectée dans ses airs, fausse dans ses virtues, intéressée dans ses libéralités, hypocrite dans ses épargnes; toujours rusée; toujours équivoque et toujours une contrevérité: du plus ou moins, voilà comme les femmes sont faites.*

11. Michèle Crampe-Casnabet, 'A Sampling of 18th-Century Philosophy' in Natalie Zemon Davies and Arlette Farge (eds), *A History of Women in the West*, vol. 3, *Renaissance and Enlightenment Paradoxes* (Cambridge, MA 1994), pp. 315–47; Olwen Hufton, *The Prospect Before Her: A History of Women in Western Europe*, vol. I, *1500–1800* (London, 1995), pp. 432–3.

12. Paule-Marie Duhet et Madeleine Ribérioux, *1789. Cahiers de doléances des femmes, et autres textes* (Paris, 1989); Marquis de Condorcet, *Sur l'admission des femmes au droit de cité* (1790); Olympe de Gouges, *Les droits de la femme* (1791); Mary Wollstonecraft, *Vindication of the Rights of Women* (1792); Sara E. Mezler and Leslie W. Rabine, *Rebel Daughters: Women and the French Revolution* (Oxford,1992).

13. Michelle Perrot, 'Roles and Characters' in Michelle Perrot (ed.), *A History of Private Life*, vol. IV: *From the Fires of Revolution to the Great War* (Cambridge, MA 1990), pp. 167–85; Pamela Pilbeam, *Republicanism in Nineteenth-Century France* (London, 1995), pp. 172–4; Anne-Marie Käppeli, 'Feminist Scenes' in Geneviève Fraisse and Michelle Perrot (eds), *A History of Women in the West*, vol. 4: *Emerging Feminism from Revolution to World War* (Cambridge, MA 1993), pp. 482–7; Hufton, *The Prospect Before Her*, pp. 25–58.

14. Gerda Lerner, *The Creation of Feminist Consciousness: From the Middle Ages to 1870* (Oxford, 1993), p. 17. See also Barbara Newman, *From Virile Woman to Woman Christ: Studies in Medieval Religion and Literature* (1995), pp. 2–3.

15. Ultramontanism fostered papal supremacy rather than the independence of national churches. In France it was expressed during the first half of the nineteenth century in papalism, a romantic interest in early Christian Rome and an idealisation of the Middle Ages.

16. Joseph-Désiré Varin d'Ainville was born into a legal family in Besançon in 1769. He decided early in life to become a priest and at the age of fifteen entered the seminary of Saint Sulpice in Paris, where he came under the influence of the rector, Jacques-André Emery. For further information on Varin's career and his association with Sophie Barat, see Kilroy, *Madeleine Sophie Barat*.

17. André Rayez et Louis Fèvre, *Foi Chrétienne et vie consacrée. Clorivière aujourd'hui* (Paris, 1971), pp. 118–22; André Rayez, 'Clorivière et les Pères de la Foi', in *Archivium Historicum Societatis Iesu*, vol. xxi (1952), pp. 300–28.

18. P. Fidèle de Grivel, 'Breve Ragguaglio de Principj e Progressi della Società del Sacro Cuore di Gesú, 18 à 20. Récit de la première inspiration du P. De Tournély concernant l'Institut féminin voué au Sacré-Cœur.' Original text and translation in Jeanne de Charry, *Histoire des Constitutions de la Société du Sacré Cœur. La Formation de l'Institut*, 3 vols (Rome, 1975) ii, *Textes*, no. 1, pp. 1–7. Also, *Notice sur . . . Léonor François de Tournély et sur son oeuvre La Congrégation des Pères du Sacré Cœur* (Vienne, 1886), pp. 104–112.

19. On attempts by Ward and others to establish an active apostolate for women, see Ruth Liebowitz, 'Virgins in the Service of Christ: The Dispute over an Active Apostolate for Women during the Counter-Reformation' in Eleanor McLaughlin and Rosemary Ruether (eds), *Women of Spirit* (New York, 1979), pp. 132–51.

20. *Notice sur . . . Léonor François de Tournély*, pp. 34–8. Merry E. Weisner, *Women and Gender in Early Modern Europe* (Cambridge, 1995), pp. 197–9, 213; Hufton, *The Prospect Before Her*, pp. 39, 379–80.

21. For the links between de Tournély's original concept, the Dilette de Gesù and the Daughters of the Sacred Heart of Jesus, see Kilroy, *Madeleine Sophie Barat*, pp. 26–48.

22. A monstrance is an ornamented receptacle in which the Blessed Sacrament is exposed in Catholic churches for the adoration of believers.

23. Pauline Perdrau, *Les loisirs de l'Abbaye* (Rome, 1934), pp. 422–4. Original text: *La première idée que nous avons conçue de la forme à donner à la Société a été de réunir le plus possible de véritables adoratrices du Cœur de Jésus Eucharistie . . . Au sortir de la terreur et des abominations de la Révolution vis-à-vis de la religion et du Saint-Sacrement . . . tout les cœurs battaient à l'unisson. Venger Jésus-Christ au Saint-Sacrement de l'autel était un cri de ralliement . . . Deux personnes pieuses ne causaient pas ensemble sans chercher quelques moyens à faire revivre Jésus-Christ dans les familles. Me voici à l'idée primordiale de notre petite Société du Sacré Cœur , celle de me réunir à des jeunes filles pour établir* une petite communauté qui, nuit et jour, adorerait le Cœur de Jésus outragé dans son amour eucharistique; *mais, me disais-je, quand nous serons vingt-quatre religieuses en état de nous remplacer sur un prie-Dieu pour entretenir* l'adoration perpétuelle, *ce sera* beaucoup, *et bien peu pour un si noble but . . . Si nous avions de* jeunes élèves *que nous formerions à l'esprit d'adoration et de réparation, que se serait différent ! et je voyais des centaines, des milliers d'adoratrices devant un* ostensoir idéal, universel, élevé au-dessus de l'église. *C'est cela disais-je, devant un saint Tabernacle solitaire: il faut nous vouer à l'éducation de la jeunesse; refaire dans les âmes les fondements solides d'une foi vive au Très Saint Sacrement, y combattre les traces du jansénisme qui a amené l'impiété et, avec les révélations de Jésus-Christ à la Bienheureuse Marguerite-Marie sur la dévotion réparatrice et expiatrice envers son Cœur Sacré au Très Saint Sacrament, nous élèverons une foule d'adoratrices de toutes les nations jusqu'aux extrémités de la terre.* Margaret Mary Alacoque ('Blessed Margaret Mary') (1647–90), visionary and member of the Visitation Order, promoted and popularised the cult of the Sacred Heart. She was canonised in 1920.

24. *Vie de Madame Geoffroy* (Poitiers, 1854).

25. Although the Jesuits had been suppressed in France in 1763, many of them continued to serve quietly in parishes.

26. *Vie de Madame Geoffroy*, p. 17. Original text: '*Celle qui est destinée à être en France la fondatrice de cette congrégation est encore occupée du soin de ses poupées.*' Sophie never commented on this and omitted this phrase from her Journal de Poitiers.

NOTES TO ROSEMARY RAUGHTER

1. Nano Nagle to Teresa Mulally, 21 Aug. 1777, in T.J. Walsh, *Nano Nagle and the Presentation Sisters* (Dublin, 1959), pp. 357–8. 'An establishment of this Society in the metropolis' refers to both women's desire to establish a foundation of the Society of the Charitable Instruction in Dublin.

2. On the emergence of the new religious orders and the experience of women during the Counter-Reformation see Ruth Liebowitz, 'Virgins in the Service of Christ: The Dispute over an Active Apostolate for Women during the Counter-Reformation' in Eleanor McLaughlin and Rosemary Ruether (eds), *Women of*

Spirit (New York, 1979), pp. 132–51; and Olwen Hufton, *The Prospect Before Her: A History of Women in Western Europe, 1500–1800* (London, 1995), pp. 373–85. Angela Merici founded the first Ursuline congregation in 1535, Jeanne de Chantal founded the Visitation Order in 1610 and Mary Ward established the Institute of the Blessed Virgin Mary in 1622. All these organisations were initially unenclosed: members took simple vows and were committed to an active apostolate. However, enclosure was subsequently imposed on both the Ursuline and the Visitation Orders, while Ward's Institute was dissolved by the Pope in 1631 and received papal approval only in 1703.

3. On the condition of Irish Catholicism during this period see Maureen Wall, *The Penal Laws, 1691–1760* (Dundalk, 1961); and James Kelly, 'The Impact of the Penal Laws', in James Kelly and Daire Keogh (eds), *History of the Catholic Diocese of Dublin* (Dublin, 2000), pp. 144–74.

4. On the 'domestic' quality of Irish Catholicism see Patrick J. Corish, 'Women and Religious Practice' in Margaret MacCurtain and Mary O'Dowd (eds), *Women in Early Modern Ireland* (Dublin 1991), pp. 212–20. On the concept of a 'matriarchal era' see J. Bossy, *The English Catholic Community, 1570–1850* (London, 1975), pp. 153–60.

5. On this movement see Rosemary Raughter, 'A Natural Tenderness: The Ideal and the Reality of Eighteenth-Century Female Philanthropy' in Maryann Gialanella Valiulis and Mary O'Dowd (eds), *Women and Irish History* (Dublin, 1997), pp. 71–88.

6. Sarah Trimmer, *The Oeconomy of Charity, or an Address to Ladies* (Dublin, 1787), p. 19; *Reports of the Society for Promoting the Comforts of the Poor*, vol. I (Dublin, 1800), pp. 69–70.

7. On the Nagle sisters' almsgiving see Walsh, *Nano Nagle*, pp. 41–2; on the impact on Nano of her encounters with the poor see Dr Coppinger, *The Life of Miss Nano Nagle* (Cork, 1794) p. 387.

8. Professor Alfred O'Rahilly (ed.), 'A Letter about Miss Mulally and Nano Nagle', *Irish Ecclesiastical Record* (1932), fifth series, XL, 474–81, 612–24, 620–21.

9. Joseph O'Carroll, 'Contemporary Attitudes towards the Homeless Poor, 1725–1775', in David Dickson (ed.), *The Gorgeous Mask: Dublin, 1700–1850* (Dublin, 1987), pp. 64–85; Raughter, 'A Natural Tenderness', pp. 72, 87; Maria Luddy, *Women and Philanthropy in Nineteenth-Century Ireland* (Cambridge, 1995).

10. Coppinger, *Life*, p. 26.

11. Teresa Mulally to Archbishop Troy, undated but probably 1802, MS, Archives of Presentation Convent, George's Hill, Dublin.

12. Coppinger, *Life*, p. 26.

13. MS Annals of the Sisters of Charity, Sisters of Charity Archives, Milltown, Dublin; Patrick Cunningham (ed.), 'The Catholic Directory for 1821', *Reportorium Novum* (1960) 11:2, pp. 324–63. For an account of Bridget Burke see Matthew Davenport Hill, *Our Exemplars, Poor and Rich* (London, 1861), pp. 95–109.

14. 'Address to the Charitable of St Michan's Parish', 1766, MS, Presentation Archives, George's Hill.

15. Annals of the Presentation Convent, George's Hill, MS, Presentation Archives, George's Hill; Subscription List, 1766–72, in Respect of the School for Poor Girls

at Mary's Lane, MS, Presentation Archives, George's Hill; Roland Burke Savage, *A Valiant Dublin Woman: The Story of George's Hill* (Dublin, 1940), pp. 60, 66.

16. Annals, George's Hill; Subscription List, 1766–72; on social backgrounds of Mulally, Corballis and Clinch see Burke Savage, *A Valiant Dublin Woman*, pp. 49–52, 64.

17. Walsh, *Nano Nagle*, pp. 28–30.

18. Ibid., pp. 62–3.

19. 'An Outline of the Lineage and Virtues of Our Respected Foundress', MS, South Presentation Convent, Cork; Walsh, *Nano Nagle*, pp. 154–5.

20. Burke Savage, *A Valiant Dublin Woman*, p. 53.

21. Davenport Hill, *Our Exemplars*, pp. 95–109; Cunningham, 'Catholic Directory', p. 333.

22. On confraternities in western Europe see Louis Chatellier, *The Europe of the Devout: the Catholic Reformation and the Formation of a New Society* (Cambridge, 1989), p. 141; also Kathryn Norbert, *Rich and Poor in Grenoble, 1600–1814* (London, 1985), pp. 20–1. On confraternities in Ireland see Register of the Confraternity of the Cord of St Francis, Wexford, 1763–1834, MS C342, Franciscan Library, Killiney; Rev. Francis Walsh, *Funiculus Triplex, or The Indulgences of the Cord of St Francis* (Dublin, 1797), pp. 101–6; Rev. John MacErlean, *The Sodality of the Blessed Virgin Mary in Ireland* (Dublin, 1928), pp. 11, 13, 14, 17, 19; Myles V. Ronan, *An Apostle of Catholic Dublin* (Dublin, 1944), p. 123; Kelly, '*The Impact of the Penal Laws*', p. 146; Kevin Whelan, 'The Catholic Community in Eighteenth-Century County Wexford', in T.P. Power and Kevin Whelan (eds), *Endurance and Emergence: Catholics in Ireland in the Eighteenth Century* (Dublin 1990), p. 150.

23. Nano Nagle to Miss Fitzsimons, 17 July 1769, in Walsh, *Nano Nagle*, p. 345 Coppinger, *Life*, p. 7.

24. Nagle to Fitzsimons, 17 July 1769, in Walsh, *Nano Nagle*, p. 346.

25. Nagle to Fitzsimons, early 1770, in Walsh, *Nano Nagle*, pp. 347–8; Nagle to Fitzsimons, 17 July 1769, p. 347.

26. 'Rules Observed in the Schools for Poor Girls which Began in 1766 in Mary's Lane', MS, Presentation Archives, George's Hill.

27. Nagle to Fitzsimons, early 1770, in Walsh, *Nano Nagle*, p. 348; Nagle to Fitzsimons, 17 July 1769, p. 346.

28. 'Address to the Charitable'.

29. Teresa Mulally to Archbishop Troy, Dublin, undated, MS, Presentation Archives, George's Hill.

30. Nagle to Fitzsimons, 28 Sept. 1770, in Walsh, *Nano Nagle*, p. 355.

31. Nagle to Fitzsimons, 17 July 1769, Ibid., p. 345.

32. Patrick Corish, *The Catholic Community in the Seventeenth and Eighteenth Centuries* (Dublin, 1981), pp. 123–4.

33. Walsh, *Nano Nagle*, p. 84.

34. Ibid., p. 85.

35. Nagle to Mulally, Cork, 29 July 1780, in Walsh, *Nano Nagle*, p. 364.

36. *A Valiant Dublin Woman*, pp. 94–5, 165–6.

37. Ibid., pp. 112, 185–7.

38. 'A Letter about Miss Mulally and Nano Nagle', pp. 619, 621; *A Valiant Dublin Woman*, pp. 119–25.

39. Nagle to Fitzsimons, 17 July 1769, in Walsh, *Nano Nagle*, p. 345.
40. Coppinger, *Life*, pp. 18, 23.
41. Nagle to Fitzsimons, Bath, 20 July 1770, in Walsh, *Nano Nagle*, p. 353. The letter is mutilated and Nano's reasons for rejecting Butler's advice are unclear. According to Walsh (p. 69), 'she had determined views against seeking approbation from the ascendancy when Catholic principles were involved'. However, she was clearly also anxious to avoid attracting attention: as she remarks in the same letter, 'the less noise is made about affairs of this kind . . . the better'.
42. Davenport Hill, *Our Exemplars*, p. 101.
43. Luddy, *Women and Philanthropy*, p. 35; also pp. 21–3, 35–45, 215–16.
44. Sister Mary Genevieve OP, 'Mrs Bellew's Family in Channel Row', *Dublin Historical Record* (1968), 22, pp. 230–41; John Kingston, 'The Carmelite Nuns in Dublin, 1644–1829', *Reportorium Novum* (1964), 3:2, pp. 331–60; Kelly, 'The Impact of the Penal Laws', pp. 153, 157, 169.
45. See Liebowitz, 'Virgins in the Service of Christ', pp. 132–51; and Hufton, *The Prospect Before Her*, pp. 373–85.
46. Presentation Annals, quoted in Walsh, *Nano Nagle*, p. 99.
47. Caitriona Clear, 'The Limits of Female Autonomy: Nuns in Nineteenth-Century Ireland', in Maria Luddy and Cliona Murphy (eds), *Women Surviving: Studies in Irish Women's History in the 19th and 20th Centuries* (Dublin, 1989), pp. 15–50, pp. 28–9.
48. Mother Angela Collins to Miss Mulally, 31 March 1786, in Walsh, *Nano Nagle*, p. 370.
49. Nagle to Mulally, 24 Aug. 1778, ibid., p. 359.
50. Dr Moylan to Dr Troy, 7 Nov. 1788, ibid., pp. 372–3.
51. Ibid., pp. 95–6. According to the Annals, Nagle stated that 'if he was pleased to drive her thence she . . . would retire to some other part of Ireland, where she would meet with no opposition and more encouragement . . . Not willing to . . . hand over to another diocese a treasure which was so much wanted in Cork he [Moylan] remained ever after silent on the subject.'
52. Annals, Presentation Archives, George's Hill; Walsh, *Nano Nagle*, p. 166.
53. Walsh, *Nano Nagle*, p. 173.
54. Clear, 'The Limits of Female Autonomy', p. 31.
55. Hufton, *The Prospect Before Her*, p. 392.

NOTES TO SUELLEN HOY

1. Leslie Woodcock Tentler, 'On the Margins: The State of American Catholic History', *American Quarterly*, 45, March 1993, p. 108.
2. My husband, Walter Nugent, then Andrew V. Tackes Professor of American History at the University of Notre Dame, held the Mary Ball Washington Chair at University College Dublin during 1991–92. For quotations see Hasia R Diner, *Erin's Daughters in America: Irish Immigrant Women in the Nineteenth Century* (Baltimore, MD: Johns Hopkins University Press, 1983), p. 130; Ellen Skerrett (ed.), *At the Crossroads: Old Saint Patrick's and the Chicago Irish*, (Chicago, IL:

Loyola Press, 1997), p. xiii; see also Suellen Hoy, 'The Journey Out: The Recruitment and Emigration of Irish Religious Women in the United States, 1812–1914', *Journal of Women's History*, 6/7, Winter/Spring 1995, 64–98.

3. William J. Onahan, *A Little History of Old Saint Mary's Church, Chicago* (privately published, Chicago, 1908), p. 24.

4. Ellen Skerrett, 'Chicago's Irish and "Brick and Mortar Catholicism": A Reappraisal', *US Catholic Historian*, 14, Spring 1996, p. 54. Skerrett explains the appeal of 'brick and mortar Catholicism', and shows how it had 'long-term positive consequences for individual congregations and the larger city'. For a similar perspective see Kathleen Neils Conzen, 'Forum: The Place of Religion in Urban and Community Studies', *Religion and American culture*, 6, Summer 1996, pp. 108–14.

5. Mother Mary Austin Carroll RSM, *Leaves from the Annals of the Sisters of Mercy in Four volumes*, vol. 3: *Containing Sketches of the Order in Newfoundland and the United States*, (New York: Catholic Publication Society, 1889), p. 245.

6. Sister Agatha O'Brien to Sister Gertrude Gibbons, 12 Nov. 1850, Sisters of Mercy Archives, Chicago.

7. Lawrence J. McCaffrey, 'The Irish-American Dimension' in Lawrence J. McCaffrey, Ellen Skerrett, Michael F. Funchion and Charles Fanning, *The Irish in Chicago*, (Urbana, IL: University of Illinois Press, 1987), p. 1. See also McCaffrey's 'Conclusion', p. 146.

8. On Catherine McAuley's advice to 'go out quickly' to the poor see Sister Mary Carmel Bourke RSM, *A Woman Sings of Mercy: Reflections on the Life and Spirit of Mother Catherine McAuley, Foundress of the Sisters of Mercy*, (Sydney: E.J. Dwyer 1987), p. 8; for the term 'walking nuns' see Sister M. Angela Bolster RSM, *Catherine McAuley: Venerable for Mercy*, (Dublin: Dominican Publications, 1990), p. 55.

9. William K. Beatty, 'When Cholera scourged Chicago', *Chicago history*, xl, Spring 1982, p. 8; Joy Clough RSM, *In Service to Chicago: The History of Mercy Hospital* (Chicago: Mercy Hospital, 1979), p. 18. Sister Agatha knew the risks of taking over the hospital, but they did not stop her. In a letter, she wrote: 'I am fearful and uneasy because an Hospital is such an arduous undertaking, but if Heaven aids us all will be right.' Sister Agatha O'Brien to Sister Scholastica Drum, 7 Feb. 1851, Mercy Archives.

10. These quotations are taken from five letters written by Sister Agatha O'Brien on 12 Nov. 1850; 7 Feb. 1851; 28 June 1851; 4 Sept. 1851; and 12 Nov. 1851, Mercy Archives.

11. Sister Agatha O'Brien died on 8 July 1854, after a full day of nursing. By 11 July three more nuns – all born in Ireland – had also become cholera victims. Later that year, in December, when the Sisters of Mercy opened their second Chicago academy, it bore the name of St Agatha as a tribute to their young leader from County Carlow. For more on Chicago's first Catholic sisters see Suellen Hoy, 'Walking Nuns: Chicago's Irish Sisters of Mercy' in Skerrett (ed.), *At the Crossroads*, pp. 39–51, 139–44. Jane Addams was born on 6 September 1860 in a small town, Cedarville, in north central Illinois; she lived until 1935. Ellen Gates Starr was born on 19 March 1859 on a farm near Laona, Illinois. In 1920 she was converted to Catholicism; she died in 1940 at the Convent of the Holy Child in Suffern, New York, where she had lived as an Oblate of St Benedict. It

should be known that she was the niece of Eliza Allen Starr, one of Chicago's foremost Catholic converts. Starr had 'the greatest childhood influence on Ellen', and always considered the Sisters of Mercy her 'old and true friends'. See Allen F. Davis, 'Ellen Gates Starr', in Edward T. James et al. eds., *Notable American Women, 1607–1950: A Biographical Dictionary*, vol. 3 (Cambridge, MA: Belknap Press of Harvard University, 1971), pp. 351–53; Rev. James J. McGovern, *The Life and Letters of Eliza Allen Starr*, (Chicago, IL: Lakeside Press, 1905), p. 169.

12. An Act to incorporate the Sisters of the Good Shepherd, of the City of Chicago, 7 March 1867, *Laws of Illinois 1867: Private Laws*, I, p. 153. For a recent article on the Good Shepherds in Chicago see Suellen Hoy, 'Caring for Chicago's Women and Girls: The Sisters of the Good Shepherd, 1859–1911', *Journal of Urban History*, 23, March 1997, 260–94.

13. A.M. Clarke, *Life of Reverend Mother Mary of St Euphrasia Pelletier: First Superior General of the Congregation of Our Lady of Charity of the Good Shepherd of Angers*, (London: Burns and Oates, 1895), p. 145.

14. These figures are taken from the manuscript federal censuses for 1860 and 1910. The three non-Irish sisters at the House of the Good Shepherd were German; at the Chicago Industrial School the four non-Irish sisters were German (three) and French (one). Mother Mary Nativity Noreau, who was born in Montreal, came to Chicago in August 1864. She proved herself a builder, despite the difficult problems she faced throughout her fifteen years as superior. After she died of pneumonia in March 1879 a group of friends and supporters resolved to complete 'the building and extension of the House of the Good Shepherd as an appropriate monument' to her memory. For reports of her sickness, death and funeral see *Chicago Tribune*, 7, 8, 10 and 12 March 1879.

15. On delinquent young women in Chicago see Mrs Joseph T. Bowen, 'The Delinquent Children of Immigrant Parents' in *Proceedings of the National Conference of Charities and Correction*, Washington, DC, 1909, p. 257. On conflicts between immigrant daughters and their parents in general see Mary E. Odem, "This Terrible Freedom": Generational Conflicts in Working-Class Families' in *Delinquent Daughters: Protecting and Policing Adolescent and Female Sexuality in the United States, 1885–1920*, (Chapel Hill, NC: University of North Carolina Press, 1995), pp. 157–84. On the lack of decent work for women in Chicago see *Chicago Tribune*, 12 Feb. and 13 April 1888.

16. On Irish bishops and priests see Jay P. Dolan, *The American Catholic Experience: A History from Colonial Times to the Present*, (New York: Doubleday, 1985), pp. 143–44; Michael F. Funchion, 'Irish Chicago: Church, Homeland, Politics and Class – The Shaping of an Ethnic Group, 1870–1900', in Melvin G. Holli and Peter d'A Jones (eds), *Ethnic Chicago*, (Grand Rapids, MI: William B. Eerdmans, 1984), p. 18.

17. Hoy, 'The Journey Out', p. 88.

18. Ibid., especially pp. 81–2.

19. For a short history of the Illinois Woman's Alliance see Meredith Tax, *The Rising of the Women: Feminist Solidarity and Class Conflict, 1880–1917*, (New York: Monthly Review Press, 1980), pp. 65–89 (quotation on p. 69).

20. The Alliance inspected the House of the Good Shepherd in 1889 and reported that it 'is a necessity, and that it is well managed . . . [O]pen-hearted and frank

explanation of every detail we inquired into . . . was given us by the mother superior' and that 'the management was everything to be desired'. Unidentified clipping, Aug. or Sept. 1889, Thomas J. and Elizabeth Morgan Collection, Book 2 (Scrapbooks), Illinois Historical Survey, University of Illinois, Urbana.

21. For the sisters' brief version see Mary Foote Coughlin, *A New Commandment: A Little Memoir of the Work Accomplished by the Good Shepherd Nuns in Chicago during a Half Century, 1859–1909*, (Chicago IL: Sisters of the Good Shepherd, 1909), p. 102. The *Chicago Tribune,* 17 and 18 Dec. 1890, has a longer version. Mother Holy Cross McCabe's statement is from an unidentified clipping, Jan. 1891, Morgan Collection, Book 2.

22. The first quotation is from Coughlin, *A New Commandment,* p. 102. The 1891 statistic is from Illinois Conference of Charities and Correction, *Handbook of Chicago's Charities,* (Chicago IL: Edwin M. Colvin, 1892), p. 80. Thomas Brenan handled the property purchase. See 'Loan to the House of the Good Shepherd/ Resolution for Members', unpublished, House of the Good Shepherd, Chicago, 17 March 1892; and *Chicago Inter Ocean,* 13 Dec. 1892. On the Donation Party see *Chicago Tribune,* 20 Dec. 1896; and [Archdiocese of Chicago] *New World,* 26 Dec. 1896.

23. In James Hurt's introduction to a recent edition of *Twenty Years at Hull House* Jane Addams and Ellen Gates Starr are described as 'fashionable young ladies' who moved to 'a dilapidated mansion in the heart of Chicago's slums determined to be "good neighbours"'. Jane Addams wrote that she and Ellen Gates Starr came to Chicago early in 1889 in search of 'a neighbourhood in which we might put our plans into execution'. They received various kinds of advice, including that of a former mayor, as they toured the city. See Jane Addams, *Twenty Years at Hull House: With Biographical Notes,* (Urbana IL: University of Illinois Press, 1990) pp. ix and 54–7. Unlike Addams and Starr Catholic sisters never 'shopped around' for a poor neighbourhood in which to work. In most instances they simply followed their own. It should be noted that the Little Sisters of the Poor had previously occupied Hull House (1876–80), where they cared for the elderly. They moved out when it became too small.

24. See Carol K. Coburn and Martha Smith CSJ, 'Creating Community and Identity: Exploring Religious and Gender Ideology in the Lives of American Women Religious, 1836–1920', *US Catholic Historian,* 14, Winter 1996, pp. 91–108 (quotation on p. 104); and Mary J Oates CSJ, 'Catholic Female Academies on the Frontier', ibid., 12, Fall 1994, pp. 121–36. In 1851, for example, Catharine Beecher pointed admiringly to the Catholic Church, which 'had posts of competence, usefulness and honour . . . for women of every rank and every description of talents'. Catharine Beecher, *The True Remedy for the Wrongs of Women,* (Boston, MA: Phillips, Sampson & Co. 1851), p. 51.

25. Marta Danylewycz, *Taking the Veil: An Alternative to Motherhood and Spinsterhood in Quebec, 1840–1920,* (Toronto ON: McClelland and Stewart, 1987), pp. 105–109. See also Hoy, 'The Journey Out', p. 84.

26. This quotation is from Mary Livermore, a Protestant reformer, who with Jane Hoge organised Chicago's highly successful Great Northwestern Sanitary Fair in 1863 during the Civil War. She became acquainted with Mercy Sisters who

nursed during that war and held them in high regard. In 1883 she suggested that Protestants might create communities of women similar to those of Catholics – they 'would furnish occupation and give position to large numbers of unmarried women, whose hearts go out to the world in charitable intent'. This quotation can be found in Sister Mary Denis Maher, *To Bind Up the Wounds: Catholic Sister Nurses in the US Civil War*, (New York: Greenwood Press, 1989), p. 39.

27. Diner, *Erin's Daughters*, pp. 139–53, for a discussion of the nineteenth-century 'world view' of Irish men and women: see especially pp. 139–40 (quotations) and 145–6.

28. Mary Jo Weaver, *New Catholic Women: A Contemporary Challenge to Traditional Religious Authority*, (Bloomington IN: Indiana University Press, 1995), p. 11.

Notes to Janice Holmes

1. *Impartial Reporter* (24 Mar. 1881).
2. Caroline Reynolds, quoted in *War Cry* (4 Sept. 1886).
3. Harold Begbie, *Life of William Booth, the Founder of the Salvation Army* (2 vols, London, 1920), I, p. 470.
4. Pamela J. Walker, 'A Chaste and Fervid Eloquence: Catherine Booth and the Ministry of Women in the Salvation Army', in Beverly Mayne Kienzle and Pamela J. Walker (eds), *Women Preachers and Prophets through Two Millennia of Christianity* (Berkeley, CA, 1998), p. 293. See also Lillian Taiz, 'Hallelujah Lasses in the Battle for Souls: Working- and Middle-Class Women in the Salvation Army in the United States, 1872–1896', *Journal of Women's History* 9:2 (Summer 1997), pp. 84–107.
5. Walker, 'Chaste and Fervid', p. 292.
6. Norman Murdoch, *Origins of the Salvation Army* (Knoxville, Tennessee 1994), p. 117.
7. Pamela J. Walker, 'Pulling the Devil's Kingdom Down: Gender and Popular Culture in the Salvation Army, 1865–1895' (unpublished PhD dissertation., Rutgers University, 1992), pp. 131–2.
8. Murdoch, *Origins*, p. 118.
9. *War Cry* (8 May 1880).
10. Ibid.
11. Ibid.
12. Ibid.
13. Most of the following statistical information is culled from the *List of Appointments 1883*, a comprehensive list of all officers who had served with the Salvation Army up to Feb. 1884. For statistics concerning the demographic makeup of the Army as a whole see Glenn Horridge, *The Salvation Army: Origins and Early Days, 1865–1900* (Godalming, 1993), pp. 80–5.
14. They were Mrs Broadhurst, Lisburn; Martha Reid, Belfast; and Mary Ann Hamilton ('Irish Kitty'), Newtownards.
15. *War Cry* (17 May 1880).
16. After initial services in the Music Hall, May Street, the Army moved to the Sailor's Lecture Hall on Dock Street: *Belfast News-Letter* (10 May 1880); *Belfast*

Morning News (10 May 1880). Caroline Reynolds, however, refers to 'the Bethel, on Craven Street' as their first venue: *War Cry* (15 May 1880).

17. For a legal description of an Army procession see the case of Beatty v. Gillbanks, *Queen's Bench Division* IX (1882), p. 309.

18. David Hempton and Myrtle Hill, *Evangelical Protestantism in Ulster Society, 1740–1890* (London, 1992), pp. 133–5; Andrea Ebel Brozyna, *Labour, Love and Prayer: Female Piety in Ulster Religious Literature, 1850–1914* (Belfast, 1999) pp. 145–50; Janice Holmes, *Religious Revivals in Britain and Ireland, 1859–1905* (Dublin, 2000), pp. 108–9.

19. *Belfast News-Letter* (12 May 1880).

20. *Impartial Reporter* (19 May 1881).

21. *War Cry* (10 Feb. 1881).

22. *War Cry* (9 March 1882).

23. *War Cry* (8 May 1882).

24. Ibid.

25. *War Cry* (18 Dec. 1880).

26. *War Cry* (24 Feb. 1881).

27. *War Cry* (15 May 1880); *Derry Sentinel* (8 June 1880).

28. *War Cry* (29 May 1880 and 15 May 1880).

29. *Derry Journal* (4 April 1881).

30. *Impartial Reporter* (19 May 1881).

31. *War Cry* (31 July 1881), p. 3.

32. *War Cry* (14 April 1883); *Impartial Reporter* (19 May 1881).

33. *Derry Journal* (3 Sept. 1880).

34. *Belfast Morning News* (10 May 1880). For other comments about accents see *Derry Journal* (4 April 1881); *Impartial Reporter* (19 May 1881): *Portadown and Lurgan News* (14 May 1881).

35. *Impartial Reporter* (21 April 1881).

36. Lewis P. Curtis, *Apes and Angels: The Irishman in Victorian Caricature* (Newton Abbot, 1971), pp. 1–22.

37. *War Cry* (9 June 1881).

38. *War Cry* (21 July 1881).

39. *War Cry* (19 May 1889).

40. *All The World* (Sept. 1902), pp. 471–2.

41. *War Cry* (4 Sept. 1886).

42. *War Cry* (22 Sept. 1888).

43. For a rather anecdotal account of the Army's early work in Dublin see Sister Katherine Butler, 'Dublin's Hallelujah Lassies', *Dublin Historical Record*, XXX, pp. 128–46.

44. *War Cry* (12 June 1880, 30 Oct. 1880).

45. *War Cry* (28 Aug. 1880).

46. *War Cry* (10 Feb. 1881).

47. Norman Murdoch argues, not very convincingly, that, given the large number of Catholic Irish in the East End of London, the conversion of Catholics was a key objective of Booth's early mission activities: Murdoch, *Origins*, pp. 79–82.

48. *War Cry* (4 Sept. 1886).

49. *Derry Journal* (4 April 1881).

50. *War Cry* (16 March 1889). Maryborough is now called Portlaoise.

51. This narrative is culled from accounts published in the *Londonderry Sentinel* and the *Derry Journal,* 1880–81.

52. Although other officers were involved in the opening of Enniskillen, their names have not survived. *Fermanagh Times* (11 May 1881); *Impartial Reporter* (17 Mar. 1881); *War Cry* (26 May 1881, 4 Aug. 1881).

53. Definitive details about the Hallelujah Army are difficult to ascertain. It seems to have originated in Ulster and may have been formed as a result of local converts disagreeing with the Salvation Army's strict prohibition of all forms of tobacco smoking. It seems to have had at least two active branches, one in Enniskillen and one in Coleraine, an overall leader, one 'General Gault', and an organisational magazine, the *Hallelujah Banner,* but little else about its origins and structure is known. *Impartial Reporter* (17 March 1881, 12 May 1881); *Fermanagh Times,* (12 May 1881). Schisms within local Army branches also occurred in England: Horridge, p. 31; conversation with Gordon Taylor, Archivist, Salvation Army International Heritage Centre, London, 18 Sept. 1995.

54. *Derry Sentinel* (8 June 1880); *Derry Journal* (6 Sept. 1880); *Impartial Reporter* (7 April 1881); *Fermanagh Times* (26 May 1881).

55. *Fermanagh Times* (26 May 1881); Robert Sandall, *History of the Salvation Army* (4 vols, London, 1950), II, pp. 193–97; Bailey, pp. 233–4. Such organized opposition was widespread in the South of England.

56. For basic crowd behaviour see Horridge, pp. 92–5; John Walsh, 'Methodism and the Mob in the Eighteenth Century', in G.J. Cumming and D. Baker (eds), *Popular Belief and Practice: Studies in Church History 8* (Cambridge, 1972), pp. 213–27; David Jones, *Crime, Protest, Community and Police in Nineteenth-Century Britain* (London, 1982), pp. 14–18. For descriptions of mob violence against the Salvation Army in England see Victor Bailey, 'Salvation Army Riots, the "Skeleton Army" and Legal Authority in the Provincial Town', in A.P. Donajgrodzki (ed.), *Social Control in Nineteenth-Century Britain* (London, 1977), pp. 231–53; Horridge, pp. 92–127; Norman Murdoch, 'Salvation Army Disturbances in Liverpool, England, 1879–1887', *Journal of Social History* 25:3 (Spring 1992), pp. 575–94; Murdoch, 'From Militancy to Social Mission: The Salvation Army and Street Disturbances in Liverpool, 1879–1887', in John Belchem (ed.), *Popular Politics, Riot and Labour: Essays in Liverpool History* (Liverpool, 1992), pp. 160–72; Murdoch, *Origins,* pp. 77–83; Lillian Taiz, 'Applying the Devil's Work in a Holy Cause: Working-Class Popular Culture and the Salvation Army in the United States, 1879–1900', in *Religion and American Culture* 7:2 (1997), pp. 195–223; Pamela J. Walker, 'Pulling the Devil's Kingdom Down', pp. 167–204; and Diane Winston, *Red-Hot and Righteous: The Urban Religion of the Salvation Army* (London, 1999).

57. *Derry Sentinel* (7 Aug. 1880).

58. *Derry Sentinel* (7 Sept. 1880).

59. The *Derry Sentinel* expresses all of these 'rights' throughout its coverage (see 8 June 1880 and 2 Sept. 1880 for particular references).

60. *Derry Sentinel* (5 Aug. 1880).

61. *Derry Journal* (3 Sept. 1880).

62. *Derry Journal* (6 April 1881).

63. *Derry Journal* (3, 6 Sept. 1880).

64. *Derry Journal* (6 Sept. 1880).

65. Henry N. Lowe, *County Fermanagh 100 Years Ago: A Guide and Directory 1880* (Belfast, 1990 reprint of original edition, 1880), p. 58; see also W.H. Dundas, *Enniskillen, Parish and Town* (Enniskillen, 1913).

66. Census of Ireland, 1881.

67. Fred G. Gordon, *Methodism in Enniskillen* (Enniskillen, 1918), p. 18; W. Copeland Trimble, *The History of Enniskillen with References to Some Manors in Co. Fermanagh and Other Local Subjects* (3 vols, Enniskillen, 1919), III, pp. 957–8.

68. Methodists on the Town Commission were identified by comparing the list of commissioners in Lowe (p. 75) with the names of eminent Methodists mentioned in Gordon.

69. The following summary and analysis are based on the events as reported in the *Impartial Reporter* (7 April 1881). On that day the *Reporter* issued a special supplement that recorded in detail the proceedings of the indignation meeting and the resolution that resulted. The 'fixed bayonets' story reappears in Gordon, p. 30.

70. *Fermanagh Times* (14 April 1881).

71. *Impartial Reporter* (28 April 1881).

72. *Derry Sentinel* (8 June 1880).

73. Letter from 'A Hater of Oppression', *Derry Sentinel* (7 Aug. 1880).

74. *War Cry* (6 Oct. 1881).

NOTES TO MYRTLE HILL

1. The name was changed in 1902 to the Women's Association for Foreign Missions, although it was still popularly known as the Zenana Mission. Back copies of the *Pink Paper* and *Women's Work* are held in the offices of the Presbyterian Women's Association, Church House, Belfast, and I am grateful to the staff there for facilitating my research.

2. For some thoughts on this aspect see Myrtle Hill, 'Women in the Irish Protestant Foreign Missions c. 1873–1914: Representations and Motivations', in Pieter N. Holtrop and Hugh McLeod (eds), *Missions and Missionaries: Studies in Church History*, Subsidia 13 (London, 2000), pp. 170–85. See also Janet Lee, 'Between Subordination and She-Tiger: Social Constructions of White Femininity in the Lives of Single, Protestant Missionaries in China, 1905–1930', *Women's Studies International Forum*, 19:6, pp. 621–32.

3. Catherine Hall, *White, Male and Middle Class: Explorations of Feminism and History* (Oxford, 1988), pp. 205–54.

4. According to the Reverend William Beatty, the new senior missionary of the Irish Presbyterian Church in India in 1865, 'a missionary's wife, if of the right spirit, must be of immense value, not merely as a companion and encourager and a nurse to him, in long and dreary isolation from all civilised society, and in times of depression and sickness, when there might be no European within miles

of him, but also an actual helper in purely mission work among women and girls of the station': quoted in G.T. Rea, *A Broken Journey: Memoirs of Mrs Wm Beatty* (London, 1894), p. 12. Note too that unmarried missionaries were often accompanied by their sisters, who could play similar roles as chaperone and helpmate.

5. See, for example, the description of the work of Mrs Fulton, 'dispensing medicine, superintending a girls' boarding school, running a weekly inquirers' class for women . . .', *The Missionary Herald* (Nov. 1898).

6. 'Dr and Mrs Christie have lost their little baby of three months old of infant cholera. There are very few of the mission families who have not lost little ones in this country.': Rev. A. Crawford, *Sketches of Missionary Life in Manchuria* (1894), p. 148. On the problems of illness and separation see also G.T. Rea, *A Broken Journey* (London, 1894).

7. Full runs of *The Missionary Herald* are held both in the library of the Assembly's College, Belfast, and in the office of the Presbyterian Historical Association, Church House, Belfast.

8. *First Annual Report of the Female Association in Connection with the Foreign Missions of the Presbyterian Church in Ireland, for Promoting Christianity among the Women of the East* [hereafter, the Female Association] (1875).

9. D.W. Savage, 'Missionaries and the Development of a Colonial Ideology of Female Education in India', *Gender and History*, 9:2 (August, 1997), p. 213.

10. Ibid., 211.

11. *Annual Report of the Female Association* (1876); in similar vein the Moderator of the Presbyterian Church, the Rev. J.L. Porter, asserted in 1875 that 'the mother's training is the main component in forming the character of the man': *Annual Report of the Female Association* (1875).

12. Ibid.

13. See Robert Barron, *Mary Barron: A Biography* (Belfast, 1915), for one example of the impact of this meeting on a young woman.

14. Maria Luddy, *Women and Philanthropy in Nineteenth-Century Ireland* (Cambridge, 1995), p. 63.

15. Ibid., see also David Hempton and Myrtle Hill, *Evangelical Protestantism in Ulster Society, c. 1740–1890* (London, 1992).

16. *Annual Report of the Female Association* (1875).

17. Ibid.

18. William Palmer Addley, 'A Study of the Birth and Development of the Overseas Mission of the Presbyterian Church in Ireland up to 1910', unpublished PhD thesis, Queen's University, Belfast (1994).

19. See Luddy, *Women and Philanthropy*; and Frank Prochaska, *Women and Philanthropy in Nineteenth-Century England* (Oxford, 1980).

20. *Annual Report of the Female Association* (1875).

21. Gillian McClelland, 'The Fisherwick Working Women's Association', unpublished PhD thesis, Queen's University, Belfast (1999).

22. Bonnie Smith, *Changing Lives: Women in European History since 1700* (London, 1989), p. 211.

23. W.E. Alexander, *Fitzroy Avenue Presbyterian Church: Past and Present* (Belfast, n.d.).

24. Such language is consistently used in the pages of *Women's Work*.

25. *Annual Report of the Female Association* (1897).
26. See James Strahan, *Mary Crawford Brown: A Memoir* (London, 1920).
27. Circulation had reached 28,000 by 1914: *Hitherto: 1873–1923* (Belfast, n.d.), p. 45.
28. I have not included Mrs Jacobs in this calculation. After serving as foreign corresponding secretary from 1888 to 1889 she left to serve as an honorary missionary in India; her sister took over the job at home: Obituary, *Bombay Guardian* (8 Oct. 1910).
29. Barron, *Mary Barron*, p. 165.
30. *Hitherto*, pp. 12–14.
31. The financial statements of the mission are included in the annual reports.
32. Most issues of *Women's Work* contain numerous ideas for, and examples of, imaginative fund-raising initiatives.
33. Such gifts are frequently acknowledged in the pages of *Women's Work*.
34. *Annual Report of the Female Association* (1877).
35. The extension of the mission into China in 1888, for example, greatly increased expenditure.
36. Edmund M. Hogan, *The Missionary Movement: A Historical Survey, 1830–1980* (Washington, DC, 1990), p. 146.
37. This was a junior edition of the church's missionary magazine.
38. *Missionary Herald* (July 1899).
39. During her long term as editor Mary Brown, whose brother and cousins served abroad, developed close links with Zenana missionaries, inviting them to her home when they were on furlough, and maintaining a regular correspondence with India and China.
40. *Hitherto*, p. 16.
41. *Women's Work* (Jan. 1910).
42. Separate women's conferences began in 1888. Until then the reports of the female missionaries were read by their male counterparts.
43. For examples of this aspect of the work see Barron, *Mary Barron*, and Strahan, *Mary Brown*.
44. Strahan, *Mary Brown*, pp. 98–106.
45. Address of the Reverend Wilson, reported in *Annual Report of the Female Association* (1878).
46. Wendy Holloway, 'Gender Difference and the Production of Subjectivity', in Helen Crowley and Susan Himmelweit (eds), *Knowing Women: Feminism and Knowledge* (Cambridge, 1992), pp. 40–74.
47. *Report of the Female Association* (1876).
48. However, the fact that most needed to earn a salary, and to raise funds, suggests that they were in the 'lower' middle-class bracket, and points to the problematic nature of such broad categories.
49. See various issues of *Women's Work*.
50. See Alison Jordan, *Margaret Byers: Pioneer of Women's Education and Founder of Victoria College, Belfast* (Belfast, n.d.).
51. Anne V. O'Connor and Susan M. Parkes, *Gladly Learn and Gladly Teach: A History of Alexandra College and School* (Dublin, 1983), pp. 36–7; Jordan, *Margaret Byers*, pp. 49–50. Victoria College achieved a particularly high record in this area: by 1903

twenty-two old Victorians were in the mission field, three had founded a girls' school in Damascus and many others were wives of missionaries.

52. G.G. Findlay and W.W. Holdsworth, *Wesleyan Methodist Missionary Society* (London, 1922), vol. iv, p. 28.

53. See, for example, *Missionary Herald* (1889, 1890, 1893).

54. See *Women's Work* (1911).

55. See *Women's Work* (1894).

56. See *World Missionary Conference* (London, 1910).

57. Jordan, *Margaret Byers*, p. 43.

58. *Medical Times and Gazetteer* 1, 31 March 1877; R.S. Allison, *The Seeds of Time: Being a Short History of the Belfast General and Royal Hospital, 1850–1903* (Belfast, 1972), p. 90; Myrtle Hill and Vivienne Pollock, *Image and Experience* (Belfast, 1993), p. 151.

59. The Annual Report of 1896, when the society was 22 years old, first mentions pensions as an important consideration. From 1903 a scheme was under way, paying 15 pounds a year towards a life insurance premium for each missionary.

60. Quoted in N.W. Taggart, *The Irish in World Methodism* (London, 1986), p. 66.

61. Before 1930 the percentage of doctors sent by the male mission was ten; of the Zenana, twenty.

62. See, for example, Kathleeen L. Lodwick, *Educating the Women of Hainan: The Career of Margaret Moninger in China, 1915–1942* (Lexington, 1995).

63. See *Women's Work* (October, 1911).

64. Stuart Piggin, 'Assessing Nineteenth-Century Missionary Motivation: Some Considerations of Theory and Method', in Derek Baker (ed), *Studies in Church History*, 15 (Oxford, 1978), pp. 327–37.

65. For example, Dr Margaret McNeill, Miss J. Rogers, Miss M. Stones, Miss E.J. Stevenson, Mrs Jacob.

66. *World Missionary Conference*, pp. 86–9.

67. Ibid., p. 149.

68. See *Report of the Female Association* (1878).

69. Entry for 7 Aug. 1901, manuscript diary of Dr Margaret McNeill, Manchuria, Presbyterian Historical Association, Church House, Belfast.

70. Diary of E.J. McCauley, Presbyterian Historical Association, Church House, Belfast.

71. *Report of the Female Association* (1888).

72. Regularly reported in *Women's Work*.

73. *Missionary Herald* (Jan. 1901).

74. V. Hayward, *Christians and China* (Belfast, 1974), p. 16.

75. Reported regularly in the pages of *Missionary Herald* and *Women's Work*.

76. Diary of Margaret McNeill.

77. Kathleen Bliss, *The Service and Status of Women in the Churches* (London, 1952), p. 115. See also Hayward, *Christians and China*, p. 17, who notes that within six years of the Boxer Rebellion the number of Protestant missionaries had risen dramatically.

78. The mission's extension into China, for example, was a result of demand, with the committee feeling that it 'dare not refuse': *Annual Report of the Female Association* (1889).

79. Addley, 'A Study of the Birth and Development of the Overseas Mission', p. 255.
80. Annie Gillespie died from dysentery after only eight months in China: *Annual Report of the Female Association* (1889). Miss Egan and Miss Balfour are said to have been weakened by overwork: *Missionary Herald* (1902).
81. *Annual Report of the Female Association* (1893).
82. Addley, 'A Study of the Birth and Development of the Overseas Mission', p. 255.
83. *Hitherto*, p. 45.
84. For examples of such cultural clashes on these issues see *Annual Report of the Female Association*, 1881, 1888, 1889.
85. Hayward, *Christians in China*, pp. 21–2.
86. See Rosemary R. Gagan, *A Sensitive Independence: Canadian Methodist Women Missionaries in Canada and the Orient, 1881–1925* (London, 1992).
87. Lee, 'Between Subordination and She-Tiger', p. 624.

Notes to Maria Luddy

1. For further information on the Project see Maria Luddy, 'The Women's History Project', in *Irish Archives* (Autumn, 1997), pp. 12–19. For a full catalogue of sources relating to women's history in Ireland see Maria Luddy et al. (eds) *A Directory of Sources for Women's History in Ireland* (CD-ROM, Dublin: Women's History Project and the Irish Manuscripts Commission, 1999). *The Directory of Sources* is also available at www.nationalarchives.ie/wh.
2. See Caitriona Clear, *Nuns in Nineteenth-Century Ireland* (Dublin, 1987); Mary Peckham Magray, *The Transforming Power of the Nuns: Women, Religion and Cultural Change in Ireland, 1750–1900* (Oxford, 1998); Suellen Hoy, 'The Journey Out: The Recruitment and Emigration of Irish Women Religious to the United States, 1812–1914', in *Journal of Women's History*, 6–7 (1995), pp. 64–98; Margaret MacCurtain, 'Late in the Field: Catholic Sisters in Twentieth-Century Ireland and the New Religious History', *Journal of Women's History*, 6–7 (1995), pp. 49–63; Maria Luddy, *Women and Philanthropy in Nineteenth-Century Ireland* (Cambridge, 1995), Chapter 2; for an account of Irish women who entered communities in England see Barbara Walsh, *Roman Catholic Nuns in England and Wales, 1800–1937: A Social History* (Dublin, 2002).
3. See Tony Fahey, 'Nuns in the Catholic Church in Ireland in the Nineteenth Century', in Mary Cullen (ed.), *Girls Don't Do Honours: Irish Women in Education in the 19th and 20th Centuries* (Dublin, 1987), p. 7.
4. Magray, *Transforming Power*, pp. 14–31.
5. MS Annals, Presentation Convent, Carrick-on-Suir, County Tipperary.
6. See Magray, *Transforming Power*, Chapter 2.
7. MS Annals, Presentation Convent, Thurles, County Tipperary.
8. See Clear, *Nuns in Ireland.*
9. For Sargent's story see M.C. Normoyle, *A Tree is Planted* (Waterford, 1976), pp. 303–4; MS Annals, 1813–1917, Presentation Convent, Clonmel, County Tipperary; 'Presentation Roots, Typescript Copy of the Annals of the South Presentation Convent, Cork', pp. 12, 14.

10. See Magray, *Transforming Power*, and Clear, *Nuns in Ireland*, for dowry requirements.

11. For further information on Nagle's work see Magray, *Transforming Power*, Chapter 2; M. Raphael Consedine P.B.V.M., *Listening Journey* (Victoria, 1983); T.J. Walsh, *Nano Nagle and the Presentation Sisters* (Dublin, 1959); Rosemary Raughter, 'A Natural Tenderness: The Ideal and the Reality of Eighteenth-Century Female Philanthropy', in Maryann Gialanella Valiulis and Mary O'Dowd (eds), *Women and Irish History: Essays in Honour of Margaret MacCurtain* (Dublin, 1997), pp. 71–88.

12. Magray, *Transforming Power*, pp. 20–23.

13. Ibid., pp. 20–23.

14. Quoted in Sr M. Angela Bolster, *Catherine McAuley in Her Own Words* (Dublin, 1978), p. 30.

15. F. Ball to Very Revd Mother, 26 Feb. 1862, Archives, Loreto Abbey, Rathfarnham.

16. Letter of Mother Mary Aikenhead to Sr Mary de Chantal, 23 June 1832, Dublin, Religious Sisters of Charity Generalate, 1/A/7.

17. *Guide for the Religious Called Sisters of Mercy* (London, 1866), part iii, pp. 109–17 and *passim*. See Clear, *Nuns in Ireland*, and Magray, *Transforming Power*, for further information on lay sisters.

18. See Roland Burke-Savage, *Catherine McAuley: the First Sister of Mercy* (Dublin, 1949), p. 363.

19. See, for example, Suellen Hoy and Margaret MacCurtain (eds), *From Dublin to New Orleans: The Journey of Nora and Alice* (Dublin, 1994); Maria Luddy (ed.), *The Crimean Journals of the Sisters of Mercy, 1854–56* (Dublin, 2004).

20. MS Register of the Acts of Election of Superioress of the Presentation Convent, Cashel.

21. See Marianne Cosgrave, 'An Introduction to the Archives of Roman Catholic Congregations of Women Religious in Ireland with Particular Reference to Genealogical Research', in *Irish Archives* (Autumn, 1997), pp. 5–12.

22. Sr M. Dominic Kelly, *The Sligo Ursulines: The First Fifty Years, 1826–1876* (Sligo, 1987), p. 9.

23. The *Annals of the Sisters of Mercy* has been reprinted by Routledge/Thoemmes Press in their series Irish Women Writers, ed. Maria Luddy (London, 1998).

24. Sr Mary Hermenia Muldrey, *Abounding in Mercy: Mother Austin Carroll* (New Orleans, 1988), p. 201. Carroll was the author of a number of works on the Sisters of Mercy: see her *Leaves from the Annals of the Sisters of Mercy*, vol. 2, *England Scotland, Australia and New Zealand* (New York, 1883); *Leaves from the Annals of the Sisters of Mercy*, vol. 3, *Newfoundland and the United States* (New York, 1889); and *Leaves from the Annals of the Sisters of Mercy*, vol. 4, *South America, Central America, and the United States* (New York, 1895).

25. MS Mother Catherine's diary, 2 July 1812 to 29 August 1825, in Archives of the Sisters of Charity, Caritas, Sandymount, Dublin. See Luddy (ed.), *The Crimean Journals of the Sisters of Mercy*.

26. It should be noted that access to records of industrial schools, reformatory schools and magdalen asylums is closed. Generally a one-hundred-year rule applies.

27. See Luddy, *Philanthropy*, Chapter 4, for further information on these refuges.

28. See Mary Purcell, *To Africa With Love: The Biography of Mother Mary Martin* (Dublin, 1987).

29. See for instance, Sharon Ouditt, *Fighting Forces, Writing Women* (London, 1992); Claire Tylee, *The Great War and Women's Consciousness* (London, 1990).

30. Papers of Miss Marie Helena Martin, Period A: 1915–1921, correspondence with her mother, letter dated 4 Jan. 1916, Medical Missionaries of Mary Archive, Drogheda.

31. Papers of Marie Helena Martin, letter dated 1 Feb. 1916.

32. Member of the Congregation, *The Life and Work of Mary Aikenhead* (London, 1925), pp. 146–70.

33. Sr M. Angela Bolster, *Mercy in Cork, 1837–1987* (Cork, 1987), pp. 24–5.

34. *Annual Report of the Poor Law Commissioners, 1854*; see also Maria Luddy, '"Angels of Mercy": Nuns as Workhouse Nurses, 1861–1898', in Elizabeth Malcolm and Greta Jones (eds), *Medicine, Disease and the State in Ireland, 1650–1940* (Cork, 1999), pp. 102–117.

35. *Irish Poor Law Intelligence*, 16 Oct. 1895; *Return of All Workhouses in Ireland in which Nuns are Engaged as Nurses*, HC 1873 (246), lv, 865.

36. For discussions regarding the entrance of the Sisters of Mercy into the Ennis workhouse see *Clare Journal*, 8, 15 May, 5 and 19 June, and 3 July, 1884.

37. Quoted from the Annals in Sr Pius O'Brien, *The Sisters of Mercy of Ennis* (Killaloe, 1992), pp. 70–1.

38. *Guide for the Religious Called Sisters of Mercy* (Dublin, 1866), p. 42. For an account of how nuns dealt with patients who suffered from frostbite, typhus and cholera in the Crimea see M. Aloysius Doyle, *Memories of the Crimea* (London, 1897).

39. Among papers in an uncatalogued collection in box III C. Workhouses – Reforms. Elphin Diocesan Archives, Sligo.

40. The archives of the Dominican Order in Dublin have been listed by Sr Dominic Horgan and the consultant archivist Marianne Cosgrave; *Weavings: Celebrating Dominican Women* (Dublin, n.d.).

41. F. Ball to Revd M.M. Teresa, 29 Nov. 1851, Archives Loreto Abbey, Rathfarnham, Dublin.

42. Annals of the Sisters of Mercy, Kilrush, quoted in Sr Pius O'Brien, *The Sisters of Mercy at Kilrush and Kilkee* (Ennis, 1997), pp. 34–5.

NOTES ON CONTRIBUTORS

Myrtle Hill is currently Director of the Centre for Women's Studies at Queen's University, Belfast. A senior lecturer in social, religious and women's history, she has published widely in these areas. Her books include *Women in Ireland: A Century of Change* (2003), *The Time of the End: Millenarian Beliefs in Ulster* (2001); (with V. Pollock) *Women of Ireland, Image & Experience,* c1880–1920 (1999) and (with David Hempton) *Evangelical Protestantism in Ulster,* 1740–1900 (1992). Recent articles on feminism and women's history include: 'Challenging the State We're In: The Feminist Seventies in "Troubled" Northern Ireland', Helen Graham, Ann Kaloski, Ali Neilson and Emma Robertson (eds), *The Feminist Seventies* (2003), pp. 75–90; 'Re-visioning Women's Studies', *Feminist Theory,* Vol. 4 (3) December, 2003, pp. 355–8; 'Lessons and Legacies: Feminist Activism in the North, c1970–2000, *Women's Studies Review,* Vol. 9, 2004, pp. 135–150; 'Reflecting on Re-presentations: Writing the History of 20th Century Irishwomen', *Women's History Magazine,* 47, Summer 2004, pp. 4–10; 'Women to Women: the role of Irishwomen in Protestant foreign missions, 1874–1914', *Subsidiary to Studies in Church History,* Winter 2000, pp. 170–85.

Janice Holmes was educated at the University of Windsor, the University of Guelph and Queen's University at Kingston, where she completed an MA dissertation in 1991 on the 1859 Ulster Revival. As the recipient of a Queen's Belfast Exchange Scholarship, she studied at Queen's University, Belfast 1990–91, and enrolled there for a PhD, under the supervision of Professor David Hempton. Her dissertation, an exploration of the nature of religious revivals in late-Victorian Britain and Ireland, was completed in 1995 and published in 2000 under the title *Religious Revivals in Britain and Ireland, 1859–1905.* In 1994 she was appointed a Faculty of Arts Fellow in the Combined Departments of History at University College, Dublin. In 1997 she took up her current appointment as Lecturer in Irish History in the School of History and International Affairs at the University of Ulster, Coleraine. Since the publication of *Religious Revivals,* she has continued to work on aspects of the Irish evangelical experience and has published articles in the *Proceedings of the Royal Irish Academy* and *Historical Studies*. Her work has examined the intersection of evangelicalism and sectarian violence in nineteenth-century Belfast and the development of evangelical networks within the British Isles. She is currently working on a biography of the Reverend Hugh Hanna, a leading Belfast Presbyterian. She is a member of the Ecclesiastical History Society and has served on the Irish Committee of Historical Sciences, the Ulster Society for Irish Historical Studies and the Economic and Social History Society of Ireland.

Suellen Hoy is guest professor of history at the University of Notre Dame (Notre Dame, Indiana). She is the author of *Chasing Dirt: the American Pursuit of Cleanliness* (1995) and, with Margaret MacCurtain, has edited *From Dublin to New Orleans: The Journey of Nora and Alice* (1994). Dr Hoy's other books, with Michael C. Robinson, are *Public Works History in the United States: A Guide to the Literature* (1982) and *History of Public Works in the United States, 1776–1976* (1976). Her articles include 'The Journey Out: The Recruitment and Migration of Irish Religious Women to the United States, 1812–1914', *Journal of Women's History*, 6 (Winter/Spring 1995); 'Mother Agatha O'Brien RSM' and 'Ada C. Sweet', *Historical Encyclopedia of Chicago Women*; 'Caring for Chicago's Women and Girls: The Sisters of the Good Shepherd, 1859–1911', *Journal of Urban History*, 23 (March 1997); 'Walking Nuns: Chicago's Irish Sisters of Mercy' in Ellen Skerrett (ed.) *At the Crossroads: Old St Patrick's and the Chicago Irish* (1997); 'Illinois Technical School for Colored Girls: a Catholic Institution on Chicago's South Side, 1911–1953', *Journal of Illinois History*, 4 (Summer 2001); 'No Color Line at Loretto Academy: Catholic Sisters and African Americans on Chicago's South Side', *Journal of Women's History*, 14 (Spring 2002), and 'Ministering Hope to Chicago', *Chicago History*, 31 (Fall 2002). A collection of her essays, *Good Hearts: Catholic Sisters in Chicago's Past*, will be published in 2005 by the University of Illinois Press.

Phil Kilroy is a historian of dissent and nonconformity in seventeenth-century Ireland, and of women in Europe, 1600–1900. She is the author of *Protestant Dissent and Controversy in Ireland, 1660–1714* (1994) and her biography of the founder of the Society of the Sacred Heart, *Madeleine Sophie Barat: A Life*, was published by

Cork University Press in 2000; it has also appeared in French and Spanish. Her numerous articles on the theme of women and religion include 'Women and the Reformation in Seventeenth-Century Ireland' in Margaret MacCurtain and Mary O'Dowd (eds), *Women in Early Modern Ireland* (1991), pp. 179–196, 'Quaker Women in Ireland, 1660–1740', *Irish Journal of Feminist Studies*, Vol. 2, no. 2, December 1997, pp. 1–17, and 'The Use of Continental Sources of Women's Religious Congregations and the Writing of Religious Biography: Madeleine Sophie Barat, 1779–1865', in Maryann Gialanella Valiulis and Mary O'Dowd (eds), *Women and Irish History* (1997), pp. 59–70; she edited 'Memoirs and Testimonies: Nonconformist Women in Seventeenth-Century Ireland' in *The Field Day Anthology of Irish writing*, Vol. IV, published by Cork University Press in 2002, and has contributed an essay on Lady Anne Conway (1631–1679) to the forthcoming *Dictionary of Irish Biography*. She is currently engaged on writing a series of essays on biography and history.

Maria Luddy is Reader in History at the University of Warwick. She has written widely on nineteenth and twentieth-century Irish women's history, and her publications include *Women in Ireland, 1800–1918: A Documentary History* (1995), *Women and Philanthropy in Nineteenth-Century Ireland* (1995) and *The Crimean Journals of the Sisters of Mercy, 1854–56* (2004); she has edited (with Cliona Murphy) *Women Surviving* (1989), (with Mary Cullen) *Women, Power and Consciousness in 19th-Century Ireland* (1995) and *Female Activists: Irish Women and Change, 1900–1960* (2001), (with Jean Agnew) *The Drennan-McTier Letters, 1776–1817* (1998/1999) and was one of the editors of *The Field Day Anthology of Irish writing*, Vols. IV and V (2002). From 1997 to 2001 Dr Luddy was Director of the Women's History Project, which produced *A Directory of Sources for Women's History in Ireland*, published in 1999 as a CD-ROM, and also available at: **www.nationalarchives.ie/wh.** Maria Luddy is currently working on a study of prostitution in Ireland from 1800 to 1945.

Eiléan Ní Chuilleanáin was born 1942 in Cork and educated at University College Cork. Since 1966 she has taught at Trinity College, Dublin, where she is now Associate Professor of English and Dean of the Faculty of Arts (Letters). With her husband, Macdara Woods, and two other poets, she founded the literary magazine *Cyphers*, in 1975.

She won the Patrick Kavanagh award for poetry (for her first book), and the O'Shaughnessy award of the Irish-American Cultural Institute. She has published a number of academic books and articles as well as several poetry collections, including *Acts and Monuments* (1973); *Site of Ambush* (1975); *Cork*, with drawings by Brian Lalor (1977); *The Rose-Geranium* (1981); *The Second Voyage* (1977, revised edition 1986); *The Magdalene Sermon* (1989); *The Brazen Serpent* (1994); *The Water Horse* with Medbh McGuckian, from the Irish of Nuala Ní Dhomhnaill (1999); *The Girl who Married the Reindeer* (2001); *Verbale/Minutes/Tuairisc*, with Cormac Ó Cuilleanáin and Gabriel Rosenstock, from the Italian of Michele Ranchetti (2002); and (forthcoming) *After the Raising of Lazarus*, from the Romanian of Ileănă Malancioiu, to be published by Munster Literature Centre in 2005.

Rosemary Raughter was educated at University College, Dublin, where she completed an MA thesis in 1992 on eighteenth-century women's philanthropy. She taught women's history 1993–2001 at the Women's Education, Research and Resource Centre, UCD, and is now an independent historian. Her publications include: 'A Discreet Benevolence: Female Philanthropy and the Catholic Resurgence in Eighteenth-Century Ireland', *Women's History Review*, Vol. 6, no. 4, 1997, pp. 465–84; 'A Natural Tenderness: The Ideal and the Reality of Eighteenth-Century Female Philanthropy', Maryann Gialanella Valiulis and Mary O'Dowd (eds), *Women and Irish History* (1997), pp. 71–88; 'Women's Philanthropy in Late Eighteenth-Century Dublin', Thomas Bartlett (ed.) *Lord Edward Fitzgerald Memorial Fund Collection* (1998) pp. 82–93; '"Mothers in Israel": Women, Family and Community in Early Methodism', Diane Urquhart and Alan Hayes (eds), *Irish Women's History: New Research and Perspectives* (2003), pp. 29–42. She was a contributing editor to Vols. IV and V of the *Field Day Anthology of Irish Writing* (2002), and has contributed to *The Cambridge Guide to Women's Writing in English* (1999), to the *Encyclopaedia of Ireland* (2003) and to the *Oxford Dictionary of National Biography* (2004). She is currently editing the journal (1764–1779) of Elizabeth Bennis, one of the most significant figures within eighteenth-century Irish Methodism, to be published by Columba Press in 2005.

INDEX

Numbers in italics refer to illustrations